Editors of the
Traveller —
with the respects of
the Translator

RAILROAD ACCIDENTS:

THEIR CAUSES

AND

THE MEANS OF PREVENTING THEM.

BY

EMILE WITH,

CIVIL ENGINEER.

WITH AN INTRODUCTION,

BY

AUGUSTE PERDONNET,

GRADUATE OF THE POLYTECHNIC SCHOOL.

TRANSLATED FROM THE FRENCH,

WITH AN APPENDIX,

BY

G. FORRESTER BARSTOW,

CIVIL ENGINEER.

BOSTON:

LITTLE, BROWN AND COMPANY.

1856.

CAMBRIDGE:
ALLEN AND FARNHAM, PRINTERS

CONTENTS.

APPENDIX.

PREFACE.

BY THE TRANSLATOR.

Some months since, the work of which the present volume is a translation having fallen into my hands, and appearing to me to contain much that would be useful and entertaining to those connected with railroads in this country, and fitted to supply a public want, I have undertaken to translate it for publication.

When a great evil exists in society, the first step towards its removal, is a careful study of its phenomena and causes. It must be mapped out for the public eye. Those of its causes which are under human control must be shown forth, and the public conscience awakened in regard to them; and when this is once done, an evil that may have been deplored and submitted to, for a long period, as necessary and inevitable, is at last diminished, if not destroyed.

One of the classes of evils, which are most frequently and forcibly brought before the mind, at the present time, is that class, which goes under the general head of railroad accidents.

Accidents are defined by Webster to be, "events which proceed from unknown causes, or unusual effects of known causes." Any result, which is the natural and regular effect of a known cause, be that cause what it may, cannot be called an accident. In this light, we are persuaded that the word is greatly misapplied to the various tragic occurrences which take place upon our railroads.

Words are sometimes things; for persons, who would look upon an *accident*, as a thing to be lamented or borne with resignation, but with the production or prevention of which they had little or nothing to do, might feel differently about it, if they considered, that "those calamities which are to individuals matter of *chance*, are to the public matter of *cause* and *effect*."

Even such an examination into railroad accidents as the accounts published at the present time, imperfect as they are, admit of, shows very clearly that the causes of most of them are not only well known, but are immediately under human control; being in most cases moral rather than physical; depending on the ignorance, or recklessness of man, and not upon material causes, which are beyond the control of ordinary human care and knowledge. It is rare indeed, to find a catastrophe occurring on a railroad of which this is not strictly true.

Let a bridge break down under a heavy train, a coroner's jury decides, that the bridge was not strong enough to bear the weight, or the momentum of the weight moving at a high rate of speed. Can this be called an *accident?* It was a matter of chance, as far as relates to the particular individuals who happened to suffer; but that the bridge was not sufficiently strong to bear the weight, might have arisen from ignorance, carelessness, or false economy. It would not have been called the effect of chance, had it proved sufficiently strong; it was not an accident, that it was not strong enough.

Let a train, running on a single track out of time, run backward to avoid a collision, at a rate of speed well known to be highly dangerous,* it can hardly be called an accident that cars are thrown off the track and life destroyed, for this is the usual effect of a known cause. Let a single track be used by trains running in opposite directions, and unless their place of meeting and mode of passing each other are regulated by fixed, unalterable rules, a collision or a catastrophe of this description must sooner or later occur.

* On the Paris and Strasbourg Railroad, engine drivers are forbidden, under any circumstances, to back their trains faster than ten kilometres, or about six miles an hour. Reglement concernant les Mecaniciens and Chaffeurs, du Chemin de Fer de P. a S. 1852.

Let an undue economy, or parsimony, prevail in the maintenance of the track, let it be allowed to deteriorate below the proper standard, and in a matter so closely affecting human life, the most perfect practicable standard is the only proper one, and the giving way of a spike, the loosening of a rail, may cost the lives of many; but for all this the cause is known, and it is not an accident.

The public is too apt, in events of this nature, to attribute them to causes beyond human control, or to fix the whole blame upon some single individual, and after indulging in a burst of righteous indignation and driving him off like a scape-goat into the wilderness, to subside into its customary state of indifference. But perhaps a more careful study of the whole matter might make us condemn the individual less, by showing that the fault belongs not so much to him as to a system in which all bear a part.

The public demands to be carried at high rates of speed and low rates of fare, the stockholders wish for their dividends, and the directors desire to increase receipts and cut down expenditures, and earn a reputation for prudent and economical management.

When we consider that a bridge too cheaply built, a track kept in poor order, a general management inefficient or wanting in system, carelessness on the part of conductors, incompetence in engine drivers must, sooner or later, give rise to accidents, and that just so far as the management of a railroad is marked by any of these faults, just so far is the liability to accidents increased, we can readily see how all, passengers, stockholders, directors, and managers may be, to a certain extent, responsible for the existence or the increase of these evils.

It is easier to save money for a time, by reducing the number employed upon repairs, than by a careful oversight, to see that every workman gives a full equivalent for the wages paid, and that the work is thoroughly done. It is quite a simple form of economy to lower the standard of efficiency in the *employés* generally by lowering their wages, and it is to be feared, that the present depressed state of railroad property may induce companies to take this course. Those accidents which arise from carelessness or incompetence of *employés*, and imperfections in the track or rolling material will, under such circumstances, be likely to increase, and whenever they do, the managers of roads upon which they may occur, will doubtless be severely blamed. But let these same persons undertake to raise their fares, diminish the number of their trains, or lower their rate of speed, in order to guard against the occurrence of these very accidents, and they will be perhaps even more severely blamed.

A careful study of the causes of railroad accidents would, we are persuaded, be of benefit to all. It would show those in charge of roads the dangers they are to guard against, and their own personal responsibility with respect to them; it would show passengers how many of the fatalities occurring on railroads are justly chargeable to the carelessness of the sufferers; it might show them also, that if they would travel safely, they must pay enough to maintain the road in perfect order in all its departments; and it would show stockholders that the surest protection against accidents, which even in a pecuniary view are often so embarrassing, is systematic management and the most perfect maintenance of their road in all its details.

Judge Potts of New Jersey, in the trial of the engineer of the train at the time of the late accident on the Camden and Amboy Railroad, in charging the jury, held the following language on the legal obligations of railroad operatives.

"These dangers, — of which scarce a week passes without some example more or less disastrous — call loudly for the checking and restraining arm of justice. It is time that men assuming the high responsibility connected with the popular and almost universal mode of travel, should come to know that dismissal from employment is not the only penalty of gross negligence involving the destruction of human life; and the sooner this is understood the better for them, for it will induce greater caution — the better for companies, for it will save them from great losses — the better for society, for it will secure more safety. There is no question about the duty of courts and juries to convict and punish these offences where guilt is proved. I say guilt, for gross negligence which produces death, is guilt."

It is to be regretted that the returns of accidents in the railroad reports to the Massachusetts Legislature are so imperfect. They supply but scanty information as to causes, and any calculation based upon the number of cases reported to show the number of killed and wounded as compared with the number carried would, we are persuaded, be altogether deceptive. This deficiency is the more noticeable in returns so valuable in other particulars. Enough is shown however, to prove that the chance of injury to a passenger seated in the cars is very small indeed.

If the publication of this little work should direct attention to the subject of it, and should lead to a more careful examination into the causes of accidents on railroads, and more efficient means for their prevention, the object of the translator will be effected.

ERRATA.

Page 24, line 10 from bottom, after *spoken of* insert *as occurring.*
" 32, " 14 " " for *wedge* read *wedges.*
" 84, " 14 " " for *but* read *for.*
" 84, " 11 " " for *is* read *are.*
" 95, " 9 from top under word *Premium* erase $.
" 109, " 15 " " for *measure* read *measures.*
" 143, " 3 " " for *sways* read *swages.*

INTRODUCTION.

The construction of Railways, now so common, met at first with great opposition, especially in France. Scarcely twenty years ago, the men then in power, treated with ridicule, propositions for building these iron ways. I could furnish more than one proof of this from my own experience. The struggle in relation to them was animated and prolonged.

In 1826, Mr. Seguin obtained with difficulty permission to build a railway for the transportation of coal from the mines of St. Etienne. No one then thought it possible for these roads to be perfected so as to carry passengers; and this was excusable, for in England even, where the industrial instinct is more developed than in France, this opinion was held; but in 1830, when thousands of travellers had already passed over the road between Liverpool and Manchester, it is astonishing that faith did not spring up in the minds of the statesmen and public of France. It was, however, at that time, that I was treated as a madman for delivering at L'Ecole Centrale a course of lectures on railroads, and announcing that the invention of them would bring about a revolution like that effected by the invention of printing. The success of the St. Germain road gave the lie to the adversaries of this new mode of travel; and M. Thiers, Minister of Public Works, returning from a journey in England, was willing to admit that railroads presented some advantages for the transport of passengers, so long as their use was limited to a few short lines centering in some great city like Paris, but the public did not need great lines. "For me to ask of the chamber to give you a charter for a road to Rouen," said M. Thiers to me, when I proposed with some associates to build this road, "I will take care not to do that; they would throw me out of the tribune." "Iron is too dear in France," said M. Passy, minister of Finance. "The surface of the country is too broken," said the deputy M. Allier. "The tunnels would be injurious to the health of the passengers," said M. Arago.

Power was, however, soon to yield to evidence. Companies marched more rapidly than the administration of bridges and roads, and that had at last to follow. Great lines were undertaken. It was then denied that they could compete successfully with navigable waters in the transport of freight. Facts soon destroyed this opinion, but still the antagonists had a heavy accusation to bring against them. Travelling on a railroad is exposing oneself to great danger, and in support of this opinion the terrible accident on the Versailles road, then that at Fampoux, then that at Poitiers was cited. Nothing is more consoling however than the statistics of railroad accidents; they prove that, compared with the immense numbers passing over these roads, the number of killed and wounded is remarkably small; but even if there was but a single passenger killed, timid men, without reflecting upon the much greater danger they are daily exposed to by other modes of conveyance, would still fear the risks they incur by seating themselves in a railroad car. It cannot be disputed, that the causes which may produce accidents upon railroads are still numerous, but whoever has studied the circumstances of the different accidents which have happened upon our roads, ought to wonder that, setting aside the accident on the left bank of the Seine, their results have not been more serious. Whoever is familiar with the mechanism of, and mode of working a railroad, will be inclined to consider the rarity of accidents when compared with the number of passengers as miraculous. We cannot praise too highly those who, like Mr. Emile With, the author of this work, have employed themselves in seeking out and guarding against their causes.

If accidents are now, owing to the wise precautions taken by the companies, and the watchfulness of the government, less frequent, and less serious to the passengers, they still strike too many victims among those employed on the roads, and it is painful to consider, that in spite of these precautions and this watchfulness, a concurrence of circumstances such as that which the other day brought about the accident on the left bank of the river, may occasion most serious disaster. It is not easy to settle what means should be made use of to diminish the number of accidents. Mess. Couche and Mathias have already brought their talents to bear upon this question; and Mr. Emile With has rendered a great service to the public by coming to the assistance of the government, and the railroad companies, who are considering this question with great anxiety.

Let us pass rapidly in review the different chapters of Mr. With's book. It first treats of explosions. This kind of accident is exceedingly rare, and never takes place except while the locomotive is at rest.* This depends upon the peculiar construction of these machines. A great portion of the heat being transmitted to the water to be vaporized, by means of small tubes passing through the water, a very great thickness, and consequently great strength, so as to render rupture almost impossible, may be given to the outer shell, which is not traversed by the caloric. The steam may indeed in some cases burst the small tubes, but then there is no explosion, and the water spreading over the fire extinguishes it. The mode of draught peculiar to locomotives contributes also effectually to prevent explosions while they are in motion, for this draught, produced by the passage of steam through the chimney, becomes the greater as more steam is used, and the production and consumption of steam are always proportional to each other.

Accidents produced by running off the track are, after those resulting from collisions, the most fearful. They are occasioned by a bad condition of the track or of the rolling stock.

* See Appendix, A.

Too great care cannot be used in the construction and maintenance of the track, of the engines, and of the cars. The strength of all of these has been greatly increased within a few years.

But this is not enough. We must still be careful in the selection of good material for construction, and upon many lines this has not been sufficiently attended to. The Board of Control, who often interfere in very trifling details of construction, should, it seems to me, oppose the use of improper materials, such as chairs of white cast-iron, or rails of which the iron is too granulated. On the road from Paris to Strasbourg, a great quantity of chairs, and a certain number of rails were broken. The company stipulated in its contracts that the chairs should be of gray cast-iron, easily cut by the file. The courts, nevertheless, on the evidence of an expert, compelled them to receive chairs of white cast-iron. The Board of Control might in this instance have prevented a decision, which compromised the safety of the passengers.

It is also of the greatest importance, in order that the track may be solid, that the road-bed which supports it should be perfectly dry. It is necessary then, at any cost, to procure ballast of good quality, and to secure the discharge of water by means of ditches sufficiently deep and suitably placed.

On the Versailles road, (on the right bank,) the working of the road has been suspended and the track taken up, in order to replace the clay in the road-bed with ballast of a better quality.

The rolling stock of railroads has been improved

even more than the road-bed and track. Breaking of portions of the engines and cars have become more and more rare, and their effects less injurious. It would be imprudent however not to examine them frequently, and to replace those which seem through use to have lost a portion of their strength. I do not agree, however, with Mr. With, who advises frequent testing, which seems to me to diminish the strength of the material.

The choice of manufacturers is essential. There are certain shops whose reputation is perfectly established. These should be employed even at an increased expense.

The most serious results upon railroads are caused by collisions. They may occur upon single track roads between trains travelling in opposite directions; or either upon single or double track roads, between trains going in the same direction, the second train going at a higher rate of speed than the first. There may also be a collision between a train and any fixed object upon the track, as a carriage upon a grade crossing, or cars at a station.

Collisions between trains running in opposite directions are the most terrible, but they can only occur upon single track roads, and they may be prevented by proper organization of the service, and a good system of signals. After the accident at Poitiers, on a part of the road where there was no double track, the public was needlessly alarmed at the dangers incident to single track roads, and it was even proposed to suppress them entirely.

But to do away with single track roads would deprive of a great improvement in travelling, a great number of places where the business is not extensive enough to warrant the construction of a double track. In Belgium, millions of passengers are carried on these roads without a single collision, and in Germany, where the roads are almost all single track, these accidents are less frequent than in England, where they are double.

Collisions upon single track roads can be easily avoided, where the trains are not too frequent, if certain precautions are taken, as they are upon German roads.

Collisions between two trains, going in the same direction, are less dangerous than those of which we have been speaking. The shock is much less violent. There is no other mode of avoiding them, than a proper organization of the service, and the use of the telegraph.

There is still much to desire in regard to watching upon most of the great lines. The night watch is especially imperfect. Superintendents of roads should be very strict in this particular.

Grade crossings are almost without danger, when they are so placed as to be seen from a distance; but they should not, where it can be avoided, be placed at the mouth of cuts, and especially in cuts where the line is curved. On many lines they are much too common. It has not been sufficiently considered that in many places the interest on the cost of a crossing under or over the railroad, would be less than the interest on the cost of the grade-crossing, added to the salary of a watchman.

Out of ten collisions between trains and objects standing on the track nine are occasioned by a wrong position of a switch. These switches often lead a train, which should keep upon the main track, upon the side track, where it dashes against cars standing there. On double track roads, these accidents may be prevented, by always placing the switch at one end only of the side track, so that trains on the main track must back down to it. This makes more trouble, but gives very great security. On the Strasbourg road we are governed by this rule, and there is no side track there which is not entered in a different direction from that which the train follows while on the main track. On the Northern and on the Lyons railroads, on the contrary, trains go directly upon the side track; this appears to me dangerous.

A good organization of the service, a good system of telegraph, and the most severe rules, will fail of producing the desired end, if the agents who execute them are wanting in intelligence or care. The choice of *employés* on a railroad is, as Mr. With remarks, of the highest importance for the safety of the passengers.

The business of the road is managed by the chief engineer, and the master of transportation. The directors appoint them. One of the principal merits of a good director, is to know how to surround himself with men of ability. In the transaction of a great business, it is impossible that the directors should watch over the details of the service; they must, therefore, place great confidence in, and give great power to the chiefs of the service, and if they do not select very intelligent and very industrious men, a great injury to the stockholders and great danger to the passengers may result from their choice. The merit of a superintendent is reflected in part upon the directors who have been able to discover and make use of him.

The board of administration, and the committee of directors are in the habit of appointing the inferior as well as the superior agents; but this nomination should be merely a matter of form. The inferior agents should be selected by those who directly employ them. It often happens that the directors oblige the superintendent to nominate certain persons, or use their influence, to keep indifferent or even bad agents in office. The principal superintendent, who feels his own responsibility, should resist this. It is not that he should entirely disregard the recommendation of the directors, who represent the stockholders, and who, on this account, have a right to claim some preference for their friends; but in no case should these recommendations prevail to the injury of the service. Favoritism is the scourge of great companies.

For certain employments of active service there should be some limit as to age; for example, for engine drivers, firemen, brakemen, conductors, — from thirty to forty-five years; and forty to fifty-five for watchmen, etc.

Some great companies, to secure good service, have established funds for assistance, and for pensions, with very good effect.

AUGUSTE PERDONNET.

RAILROAD ACCIDENTS.

CHAPTER I.

GENERAL CAUSES OF ACCIDENTS.

For some months, railroad accidents have become so common, that it seems as though science was altogether powerless in preventing them; in truth, they are always occasioned by the imprudence of passengers, the want of foresight in those employed on the road, or by a concurrence of fatal, but very natural circumstances. Nevertheless, it is consoling to think, that in spite of the frequency of these accidents, it is never impossible to prevent them by a due exercise of intelligence and discretion, as I shall attempt to prove in the following pages.

The part the press should play in these sad affairs, is not to excite, by its dramatic recitals, fear in the minds of travellers, and of agents of transportation, who are charged with such responsible duties; it ought, if it would be useful, to examine these accidents, both in their particular character, and in reference to the management of the road upon which they occur, and discuss fully the causes of these irregularities, and the means of preventing them.

At present, no methodical classification of these accidents, based upon their causes, has been undertaken, except in scientific dissertations. Separating for a time those which are due to malice, and to persons not in any way connected with the road, we shall divide them into four classes, namely: —

1st. Accidents caused by the locomotive.

2d. Those resulting from a bad condition of the track or of the rolling stock.

3d. Those which arise from neglects of the rules for running the trains.

4th. Those due to imprudence on the part of passengers or *employés*.

CHAPTER II.

EXPLOSION OF LOCOMOTIVE BOILERS.

The accident to which a locomotive is subject, while at rest, is the explosion of its boiler, which is the result of a culpable inattention on the part of the engine driver, or of a deterioration of the metal of which it is composed.

An event which took place some time since in England, may serve as an example of this.

Near Manchester, on the North-western Railroad,

there is a building in the form of a polygon, covered with slate and surmounted by a glass cupola. In the centre of this building there is a turntable for locomotives and their tenders, from which radiate twelve tracks, between which columns are placed to sustain the structure. In this building, known as the *polygon shed*, fires are kindled in the locomotives for the main road and its branches. It abuts against a square house, the second story of which is a reservoir for water, and the ground-floor serves as a reading-room to the numerous workmen in the repair shop; the reading-room opens into the engine-house.

In the month of March, 1853, there were five locomotives with their tenders in the house, and one designated No. 21, built in 1840, by Sharp and Roberts, was placed on the track leading out of the house. The fire had been lighted in the morning, as it was to draw trains through the tunnel; this was to be its first trip after leaving the repair shop, where it had been subjected to very thorough repairs and a very rigid examination.

It was the custom of the workmen on the Manchester Railroad to take their meals in this rotunda, which was always warm. On the day of the accident there were eighty persons there; many of them were already in the reading-room; every thing went on in order; the engineer oiled the engine, some workmen were talking with him, while others were seated on the steps of the platform. In the mean time the steam began to hiss, producing a sound disagreeable to the workmen, many of whom, warned by this sign, anticipated danger, without being able to explain its cause; and without knowing why it was dangerous to remain longer in the building, left it. It was the blue color of the steam escaping from the open safety-valves which gave them most alarm.

At this critical moment, instead of taking the most common precautions, the engine driver stepped leisurely on the engine, closed the safety-valves tight, and then quietly got down, to get the engine ready for starting. What could have led him to forget the most simple rules of prudence and self-preservation? That is a secret which the unfortunate man carried with him to the tomb. Scarcely a quarter of an hour elapsed before a hissing sound was heard, and some instants after a fearful explosion took place. Half the roof was raised and, falling, broke to pieces and covered the wretched workmen with fragments of wood, glass, and slate. The building was in a moment filled with steam, dust, and smoke, and when this cloud had dispersed, people came from all sides to inquire into the cause of this terrible devastation, to assist the wounded, to carry away the dead. The tender remained untouched in its position, with a part of the platform of the locomotive. The engine was thrown a distance of eighty feet from the end of the turntable, with its fire-box completely torn in pieces, and one of its driving wheels destroyed. It had six wheels, with the drivers in the middle.

It seems that, at the moment of explosion, the locomotive, in consequence of its irregular motions, had deranged the turntable, for the rails upon it no longer corresponded with those of the track. One of the workmen saw the engine advance and then throw its fragments forwards. All the bolts were torn out or broken. The rupture took place in almost all through the rivet holes. On the right side the expansive force of the steam was no less considerable; the threads of the screws were either torn off or flattened; the dome, completely torn in pieces, was thrown against four persons, who were instantly killed. The copper sides of the fire-box were bent in towards the fire; the explosion taking place not in the cylindrical boiler, but in the fire-box. Its principal effect was upon the left side, which was entirely carried away.

There can be no doubt as to the cause of this accident. A perfectly new engine could not have borne the pressure, which the engine driver had had the imprudence to produce. In a quarter of an hour, the steam, subjected to a high heat, had acquired an enormous, an incalculable force, but of which we can form some idea when we consider the injury done to the building, and the distance to which the fragments were thrown. An inspection of the surface of rupture proved that the material of the engine was of good quality, and able to resist a pressure tenfold greater than that necessary for the customary service of a locomotive.

I have designedly entered upon very circumstantial details on the subject of the explosion of a locomotive, produced by an excess of pressure. All these accidents, whether in locomotive or stationary engines, or those of steamboats, resemble each other; to cite one example is to mention all. These explosions are terrible; they leave no chance for safety;

but fortunately, they are becoming more and more rare, and as they are always the result of a want of watchfulness in testing the condition of the boiler, or of negligence, (for infallible signs, such as the heating of the bolts, the descent of water in the boiler, indicate the approach of danger,) they may be avoided by taking the most common precautions.

In other cases, this excessive pressure of steam, which causes a bursting of the boiler, is produced by an unperceived lowering of the level of the water; the fire attacks the metal directly and heats it redhot. If then, by any means, water is introduced, it comes in immediate contact with an intensely heated surface; an immense development of steam takes place instantly, and if the valves do not work very freely, an explosion is inevitable. This can only happen through a complete neglect of duty on the part of the engine driver. A glass guage indicates at all times the height of the water. If this does not work well, if any thing obstructs it, the engine driver finds on the side of the boiler a cock at the same elevation, then a second cock a little below that, and often a third, so that there is no excuse for him, if he neglects to test the condition of his boiler.

Besides an excessive load on the safety-valves, or a want of water, which are the ordinary causes of boiler explosions, there may be faults in the internal construction of the boiler, which have escaped the test of hydraulic pressure; but these faults in the bars, with the exception of a rapid destruction of a stay or a bolt by rust, do not readily produce rupture, if the valves work well.

Here is an account of accidents due to this last cause; they occurred on German railroads.

The first serious accident on a road in the kingdom of Wurtemburgh, where the rail of Vignoles with plates fastened with screws, and American engines are used, took place towards the end of 1853, after it had been open for traffic four years. An engine at a station on that part of the line which connects the roads of Baden with those of Wurtemburgh, burst ten minutes before the time for starting; the fire-box exploded, killing the fireman, and wounding many others. The engine was thrown thirty feet, and the tender was thrown off the track, but was not injured. The dome of the boiler was split into four pieces; the upper part of the boiler, upon which the safety-valves were found, was picked up six hundred and fifty feet from the place of the accident. This locomotive had run sixty-two thousand miles. The boiler had been thoroughly repaired twice, and had been subjected to the necessary tests by means of an hydraulic press, up to eleven atmospheres, double the pressure at which it was usually worked.

An examination very much in detail took place, but no clear indication of the prime cause of the accident was developed; the boiler was sufficiently full of water, and the pressure of the steam had not gone beyond the ordinary limits. We are forced to think that the stays must have yielded for a long time before the explosion, and that the angle irons in the dome were not made with proper care. From many trials on other machines coming from the same shop, it has been noticed that the stays were not strong enough for the force they had to resist.

On the Frankfort road, a locomotive, after having run twenty-two thousand six hundred miles, exploded. It had been sent to the repair shop, on account of leaks in the cylindrical portion of the boiler, and in several of the tubes. It was ready to start, the grate and the ash-pan had been closed, after the fire was covered with fresh coke. The engine remained ten minutes in this state, steam escaping freely from the valves. At the moment when the signal for starting was given, an explosion took place, with a noise which lasted for three seconds. The locomotive was thrown over on its side; the forward wheels of the tender were drawn off the track; the coupling was broken; the dome was torn completely in pieces; a piece of the boiler six feet square, and weighing five hundred and fifty pounds was torn off, and thrown horizontally three hundred and thirty feet, where it cut a post ten inches square in two; one of the hind wheels was thrown against the pillar of an engine house, which it damaged considerably. The axle of this wheel was bent.

From an examination of the locomotive after the accident, it was evident that all the internal stays had been broken and torn out with their bolts; that the copper fire-box had been bent, and the rivets had been violently drawn from the copper and iron casing; and that the wall of the dome had been broken principally in the angles. On calculating the force necessary to break the dome, from the thickness it presented, there must have been developed in the boiler a pressure of thirty-seven atmospheres. To prove more clearly that the thickness of the boiler was sufficient to have prevented the explosion, recourse was had to a direct experiment. It resulted from this, that this explosion could not have taken place except from the rupture of a brace, as the inquest decided. Besides, the surface of rupture of this brace showed clearly that it had been injured for a long time, and that the iron would have broken under a pressure less than that which produced a rupture of the dome.

The conclusions from what has been said, are, that the braces of boilers should be made and adjusted in the best possible way, and should be watched over in a most special manner. Braces weak, or badly set, bolts badly fitted, may be the causes of serious accidents. Finally, it is best to try all boilers, at least once a year, with an hydraulic press.

CHAPTER III.

CARELESSNESS OF THOSE IN CHARGE OF ENGINES.

Accidents may happen to engines while in motion. The tubes in the boiler may burst, and the water may escape into the fire-box; there may be leakages of steam; the fusible plug (*plomb de surete*) may melt; the bars of the grate may get loose, and fall upon the track; all these are known and may be anticipated. It is known beforehand, in any given case, when it is necessary to slacken the speed, to stop the train, to send for assistance; in fine, many circumstances, too numerous to mention, may present themselves, where the address and coolness of the engine driver can alone guard against danger.

Many engine drivers do not sufficiently consider the amount of destructive force which is placed in their hands, and which may burst forth, at any moment, when their attention is not completely fixed upon all the important parts of their engine.*

Very often the lives of passengers are in their hands. They dispose, at their will, of the property of the company, and every act of negligence on their part may have the most serious results. They should be deeply sensible of all this.

The following, taken from a German journal, proves this.

In January, 1854, on the Prussian part of the road from Saarbruck to Metz, two trains, each supposing the other behind time on account of a heavy fall of snow, came in collision. When the engine drivers came in sight of each other, they blew the whistles, the breaks were applied, the steam was reversed, and the men on both engines leaped to the ground without injury. The collision took place, but on account of the precautions taken the shock was very slight; but the steam, continuing to act on the pistons, drove the trains abandoned to themselves, with constantly increasing velocity in opposite directions. The passenger train stopped at last at the base of an inclined plane, and the freight train, after having traversed the side track at Saarbruck, stopped in the snow near the French frontier. The express train, coming from Paris, having been notified that the freight train had

* See note B.

passed, run into it, breaking many of the cars. No other accident took place.*

In many cases the engine driver, more active than conscientious, instead of taking the necessary means to stop the train, may jump off and escape safe and sound or with a few slight bruises; he abandons the train to its fate, while an honorable man would have remained, like a soldier, at his post, and braved the death that seemed inevitable. We are often forced to do justice to the zeal and devotion of engine drivers, with whom a sentiment of duty prevails over the instinct of self-preservation.

The great confidence which must be placed in them demands of companies to select men in whom the most perfect reliance can be placed in time of trial. To secure such men there is only one way; they should be well paid, and their prospects for the future made comfortable, from the time of their entry into the service; their rank should be raised, for the station demands robust health, and tried intelligence, training, and courage. We are far from the time, when Mr. Brunel, in his report to the Commons on a Railroad bill, said, "of two engine drivers, I would choose the one who did not know how to read." On many occasions, English juries, in their verdicts on explosions of locomotive boilers, have presented to the government requests for acts, "subjecting engine drivers to severe examinations, and demanding that they should be instructed."

There should also be means provided for assisting them, or for pensions for their families in case of ac-

* See note C.

cidents. But on the other side they should be made to understand, once for all, that at the least infraction of the rules, at the least carelessness or the slightest manifestation of ill-will, they will be instantly discharged, and declared incapable of serving upon any railroad in any capacity whatever, and the pensions obtained for themselves or their families at once forfeited.

CHAPTER IV.

RUNNING OFF THE TRACK.

The question of trains running off the track constantly excites the attention of the superintendents of the way and of the rolling stock. Both these departments should watch over, and take precautions for preventing these accidents, which have for their causes, —

1st. A bad condition of the road.

2d. A bad state of the track, either of the rails or the sleepers.

3d. Instability of the locomotive or a part of the train.

Inventors never having devised any infallible means for preventing running off the track, have applied, and are still constantly applying themselves to contrive an apparatus which shall maintain the cars at least on the track, though the engine should go off, an accident which may happen under a variety of circumstances. This apparatus is intended to detach at once, and without any manual assistance, the train from the engine; and for this purpose, a movable pin is fitted into the flange of the wheel, projecting very slightly from it. When the engine leaves the track, the flange goes over the rail and presses the pin in. A lock, like that of a gun, connects with this pin, and the cock striking directly on the coupling pin, throws it out; the engine goes off the track alone, and the cars follow the line of the rail. This supposes that the rails are unbroken, but as most generally the engine is thrown from the track on account of the rails being out of order, part of the train must go off with it. The mechanism of this contrivance is composed of thirty pieces, and requires great care to keep it in order; and there is no certainty that it will work well in any case.

A mode but little employed in stopping the cars, by means of a contrivance which detaches the locomotive from the train, and by the same movement causes sand to be sprinkled over the rails, has been used on the St. Etienne Road. In 1840, a locomotive broke the rail and ran off the track; this contrivance for detaching the train and sprinkling sand was used, and the cars remained on the track while the locomotive and its tender rolled over the slope. This contrivance demands the most constant attention on the part of the conductor; he must not abandon for a single instant the handle, and must have his eyes constantly fixed upon the locomotive; this seems to be a difficulty in the way of its use. I cannot decide upon any of these inventions; they should all be submitted to a general examination.

I have not spoken of engines being thrown off the track through malice; such cases are beyond the domain of the science of railroads.

The examination of the causes of these accidents is very delicate, and in order that it may be thorough, I must enter into some details on the construction of roads and the management of engines.

CHAPTER V.

FAULTS IN THE CONSTRUCTION OF RAILROADS.

The faults of construction comprise those connected with the excavations and embankments, the tunnels, viaducts, and bridges. Tunnels may give rise to accidents, by a portion of the vault falling upon the train or track. If any fears of this arise, the tunnel may be arched with masonry. Railroads are exposed to slides; one took place on the Southampton road for a distance of six hundred and fifty feet; these slides are often spoken of on English lines.

Viaducts and bridges are a difficult portion of railroads, and the attention of engineers has been, and is still applied to them.

There is no single system in the construction of bridges that prevails over all others. The problem to be resolved in reference to them is very difficult. Bridges of stone, of long spans, which resist the vibrations of passing trains, are very costly; the combination of wrought and cast-iron is objectionable on account of the different expansibility of the two metals; new constructions in wood are rare, not giving sufficient durability or security against fire. Bridges suspended by means of chains or cables of iron wire have succeeded on common roads. The first trial of a chain bridge at Stockton, on a road for the transport of coal, did not succeed; the experiment has not again been tried on a great scale, and a chain bridge of short span, built since, only served to confirm the faults of the system.

The falling of bridges, through faults in the foundation of the masonry, are not peculiar to railroads, and will not be considered here.

From the time when cast-iron bridges were first constructed in England, they were imitated, with a perfect infatuation, throughout Europe; and though at first restricted to common roads, were soon applied on a great scale to railroads.

Without a perfect understanding of the chances of accident to which these bridges were exposed, they were very freely employed, even in cases where the absence of stone did not justify their use. A new kind of cast-iron bridge, designed by Mr. Stephenson, was tried upon the Chester road; although fears had arisen with regard to it, it was nevertheless introduced, with some modifications, over the whole line. These bridges are composed of horizontal beams, in one piece for openings of thirty-three feet, two pieces for sixty-six feet, and three for an hundred. In the joints, these beams are united by plates fastened with screws; iron bars of different sorts bind together this series of beams.

Much opposition was raised in England to this union of wrought and cast-iron. While the subject was still under discussion, in 1847, the fall of one of these bridges in the neighborhood of Chester, after a use of some months, showed the danger of this kind of bridge. This event, which occasioned the death of many persons, induced the British government to take measures to prevent the recurrence of such accidents; it ordered that all bridges of cast-iron should be supported by wooden centres. In short spans struts might be placed.

It may be useful to enter into some details on the subject of this accident.

Opinions on the cause of the falling of this bridge are very diverse: it was maintained that the dimensions of the beams were not in proportion to their length: on the other hand, the fall was attributed to the shock, caused by the tender's going off the track, against the outer beam, after the locomotive and tender had passed over the two first sections of the beam.

The wall of the parapet was greatly injured by the tender, and the bolts, to the number of thirteen, torn out; the part of the beams consisting of forged iron was uninjured. The breaking of the other beams was the consequence of the falling of the bridge; the tender and part of the cars must have quitted the rails before arriving at the parapet; the wheels of the cars thrown into the river were found in good state with the exception of one. This was the wheel which, broken before the accident, must have caused the train to go off the track. This was the opinion of some. Mr. Stephenson states, in his report, that a few hours before the accident, he had examined all the parts of the bridge, and that nothing indicated to him insufficient dimensions or a faulty combination of parts.

The jury of inquest were not convinced by any of these reasons; they did not think that the fracture of the beam was owing to the shock of the locomotive, tender, or cars, or to a fault in the masonry; but that it should be attributed to the dimensions of the beam not being sufficient to resist trains travelling at high speed.

The jury declared further, that they should be false to their duty, if they did not express their opinion, "that no cast-iron bridge, even though strengthened by wrought iron, offers the requisite security for express and passenger trains; and asked in consequence, that her Majesty the Queen would order an examination of all similar structures, which should be prohibited entirely, or rendered so firm that they could resist flexure, to the extent of six inches, with perfect safety."

The wisdom to be drawn from this should be to subject all cast-iron bridges to a rigorous examination, and without going so far as doubling these works with centres, we might still strengthen them by means of struts, for which purpose we may use to advantage old rails, which, on account of a slight deterioration, can no longer be used in the track, but which offer all the benefits of tested iron. I have seen them applied in this way to the bridges on the Baden railroads.

Besides, to show the necessity for the measures

prescribed by the English parliament, as well as the propriety of the additional supports ordered by the government of Baden, we need only submit our bridges to a scientific examination, by observing the vibration, the verse sines of flexure, and the effect of expansion; after this, I do not think that more cast-iron bridges will be built.

Plate iron has taken the place of cast, tubes have succeeded beams and arches, and soon, I am firmly persuaded, the tubular system will be replaced by lattice-work, after the American plan, of rolled iron.

This lattice-work in iron has all the advantages, in an increased degree, of structures in plate or in cast-iron, without offering any of the inconveniences peculiar to them. It is inflexible, costing comparatively little, applicable to all localities, and presenting the advantage of allowing all the component parts, however small, to be examined without difficulty. They can also be readily got at without stagings, and covered with paint where they may have rusted, whilst in the cells of tubular bridges rust may progress unperceived until it shall have injured every piece, or until some catastrophe shall destroy these structures, ingenious and admirable for more than one reason, but by reason of the impossibility of being subjected to daily inspection, not able to give a guarantee for safety for a long period of time.

For some time iron lattice bridges have been built on the German roads, over short spans. At first there was a hesitation in abandoning the old system in favor of the new; but now all doubts on the subject have vanished; the bridge of Offenbourgh, with a span of one hundred and seventy six and six tenths feet, on the Baden road, near Strasbourg, has taken the place of a cast-iron arch, which was carried away by a freshet.

This new structure, designed by Mr. Ruppert, Engineer, is the object of general admiration. Travellers come daily from all countries to examine it, and all French tourists, who go to Germany, stop in the charming land of Baden, to see the railroad trains pass over this new transparent bridge.

The construction and working of railroads are subject, in France, to the constant oversight of the agents of the government. No earthwork, no construction in masonry or carpentry, no laying of track, can go on without authority from the government; no locomotive can be used without having been previously tested by the engineer of mines. The road having been opened to public travel, this oversight is continued; it is also exercised every day, by special commissioners residing on the spot. This mode of inspection is followed all over the continent, and France has nothing to learn on this subject from other nations. In England this supervision, very much the same in general, differs only in form; the English roads are visited on their opening only by a royal agent, who bears the title of Commissioner of Railways; and who may authorize or forbid the working of the road. Thus in 1851, many openings were delayed, the commissioners not finding the structures sufficiently strong, and having besides found the rolling stock insufficient.

Let us now consider the roads as duly inspected,

and found safe, and let us endeavor to discover how in spite of the continual repairs, they fail to present all the guarantees of a safe and convenient travel. How does it happen, that in spite of the severe and well-directed vigilance of the agents of control, in spite of the constant labor of companies, the way becomes bad, the locomotive injured? It is because, for the most part, these facts are beyond the reach of science, and because persons charged with the care of them, cannot always and at every moment visit and verify for themselves the details of the service confided to their care.

CHAPTER VI.

BAD STATE OF THE TRACK.

When a railroad is open, the embankments begin to crumble, the slope of the cuttings run down into the ditches and may fill up the way. The first thing is to raise up the track: the work should be attended to with great care, especially in the approaches to bridges, the level of which should be tested, as often as possible, with nice instruments. Most especially during heavy rains and inundations are injuries to be feared: at such times it would be prudent to put on special agents at the crossings of watercourses; to double the force of track hands, and to order those employed on the track not to quit the sections confided to their care.

A settling of the road-bed may cause the greatest danger; the track no longer being able to keep its proper position, trains must inevitably run off if means are not taken to prevent them. Too great economy is often practised in the width of embankments: the top width should be proportional to the height, in order that the breaking down of the slope may be without prejudice to the width of the road-bed; there are roads where the watchmen are obliged to place themselves on the slope to avoid being touched by the passing trains.

In order to make sure of the good condition of the track and every thing connected with it, it should be visited before and after the passage of every train. This is a measure of the last importance and is never neglected upon well-managed roads. The condition of the road-bed being determined, it may be that the rails are no longer kept in place, not so much by the absence of a solid attachment, as by a rotting of the sleepers or longitudinal sills, or by the separation of the stone blocks which have no transverse bond between them: then, at a given moment, the wheel, no longer kept in equilibrium by a sufficiently solid support, causes the rail to bend and spring out of place. There is but one thing to be done, to replace the supports, when their deterioration or displacement is perceived. A very simple mode presents itself: the sleepers should be entirely cleared of the ballast, for sinking them in the earth exposes the wood to the changes of dryness in summer and of moisture in the wet season, and greatly hastens the decomposition of the woody fibres; this covering of earth produces an effect contrary to what was anticipated at the beginning when it was the habit to cover the sleepers entirely with ballast. It was supposed that the sleepers would be placed in the same situation as piles driven into the ground under water; and that this would prevent their rapid rotting, as well as a disagreeable motion on the passage of trains. By placing the sleepers upon the ballast, they may be inspected daily, while in the other mode they must be dug out in order to be examined. They sometimes rot very rapidly, especially where longitudinal sleepers are used, which prevent the free discharge of water, and on this account this form of superstructure is objectionable.

Rails, with solid supports, if not firmly fastened at the joints, may cause an engine to run off the track. Accidents of this kind have only happened where movable joints were used, that is with rails fixed in chairs by simple wooden wedge, or rails of a reversed U. The wedge may quit the chair, when having been driven in a moist state into it, from exposure to the sun it has dried and become loose; the vibrations caused by the passing trains then shake it out, and the rail is no longer kept in line. In rails of a reversed U, the joints are not united at all: they rest simply upon a plate of cast-iron fixed with cramps; the rail sinks at the joint under the pressure of the wheel; the rail next to it becomes higher, and a balancing takes place, which causes the plate to work into the wood, and this loosens the cramps which should retain it in place. This is why we hear, upon track laid in this manner, a sort of shock at each joint, and a clinking of the plates, which strike against the cramps or bolts, or the bottom of the rails. This mode of attachment is inherent to the use of longitudinal sleepers, which have generally been given up by those who first made use of them.

The causes that produce irregularities in the track are often very trifling; whatever is done, and whatever inclination is given to the rails in order to place their axes in a line normal to the pressure, they are always subject to be thrown out of place.

To remedy these inconveniences, we must consider the point as a fracture, and fix the rails in an invariable manner by screwing or rather riveting two parallel plates against their sides so as to maintain them in the same position, and thus avoid a solution of continuity which may produce the most serious results. By this invariable attachment, trains are prevented from running off the track, the track is improved, and the wear of the rolling stock diminished. We see that it is necessary in all circumstances to consider a railroad as a machine for transport, all whose parts, however small, are intimately united. Every time that imperfections occur in this machine, the work labors, and if they are not remedied at once, serious results may follow.

CHAPTER VII.

WRONG POSITION OF SWITCHES.

A GREAT many accidents arise in consequence of switches or changes of the way being set wrong; on this account their use should be avoided as much as possible, especially upon those parts of the line which are traversed by express trains at high rates of speed. The attention of constructors has been always directed to the study of this question, which is of the highest importance on single track roads.

Switches are of two kinds, those which are worked by men, and those moved by counterweights; the safe use of one of these depends on the accuracy and intelligence of the switchman, that of the other on the play of mechanism, bringing the rail to its original position after the wheels of the last car have left it. If these switches work well, there is no danger; but a hard substance, a stone for example, falling between the fixed and the movable rail, prevents its closing in spite of the counterweight, which should not be heavy enough to crush the hard substance, for then it would be too heavy to be moved by the wheel of the car or engine. If this body is thrown between the rails, after the passage of the locomotive, by the shock of the passing train, a part of the train may follow one track, while a part goes upon the other, and thus the train is broken in pieces and thrown off the rails. This happened in England three times, during the year 1851, causing very serious accidents.

After a very careful study and comparison of both systems of switches and the mode of working them, the preference in France is given to those worked by a counterweight. It is not the same in other countries, where great difference of opinion on this subject prevails. An examination of the comparative merits of the two systems does not properly belong here; it will find its proper place in researches on the contruction and working of railroads.

CHAPTER VIII.

INSUFFICIENCY OF TRACK HANDS AND WATCHMEN.

ALTHOUGH rails firmly fixed at the joints give a great stability to the track, it is necessary that they should be carefully watched, and that none of the ordinary precautions should be neglected by the track hands, who should be stationed at distances of a mile and a quarter, on roads doing a great business, in order that their sections may be kept in perfect order.

It is always of advantage to have these men interested in the good condition of their sections. Capable men should therefore be chosen, married men are preferable, and small houses should be built for them, and a small lot of land given them, which they may use as their own. They will then get attached to this piece of land, and pass their lives there; rewards should occasionally be given them, which, though they may be small, are always encouraging; in a word, they should be treated kindly, but strictly, as I have before said of engine drivers; for these track men are the mechanics of the iron way.

In winter and at night they are often subjected to severe trials; often immovable at their posts, like iron automata, they are exposed to death by cold. Thus of all occupations, including that of the soldier, we do not find any more painful, any that demands more perseverance, more self-denial, and sometimes more intelligence, than that of working and taking care of railroads.

Even considered in a financial point of view, which is nothing when the lives of men are concerned, railroad companies will derive benefits from following the above suggestions.

There is little occasion to insist upon this point, notwithstanding its importance; for almost all railroad managers understand it; science and their own interests are constantly leading them in this direction. Funds for the relief of employés, which are being generally established, prove this.

A second part of the duty of the track hands is watching the grade crossings. These crossings are the weak points on railroads. When roads are first opened, accidents often happen upon them. If it is absolutely necessary to have them, they should be placed at right angles with the line, and should, as well as the track, be closed by gates; without these precautions accidents may be constantly expected. Sometimes, where these crossings are placed obliquely, carriages have been driven through mistake upon the track. But on the other hand, the management of these gates requires the most constant attention, and in many cases they give rise to new dangers, so that they have to be abandoned.

On the establishment of the English roads, the principle was adopted, that regularity of service was more readily obtained by mechanical means than by dependence upon the watchfulness of *employés*; these roads are generally little watched, but they are closely fenced, and grade crossings are almost entirely suppressed. The common roads are ordinarily carried over or under the track. Thus all obstructions are removed from the line, when it is completely closed from contact with the travel on the common roads. By thus separating the track from all external communication, a sufficient security is obtained, which is still more increased by gangs of workmen walking over it, who are engaged in keeping the line in order.

It would be useful to see whether this example deserves to be generally followed. In all cases the suppression of grade crossings increases greatly the ease of travel; for common carriages produce irregular pressure upon the rails, affecting their position and the fastenings at the joints. In exceptional cases, such as near stations and on private ways, grade crossings must be used; but they should be carefully watched.

CHAPTER IX.

INSTABILITY OF THE TRAIN.

It is easy to realize the injury done to the engine and cars by a bad state of the track. If a comparison may be permitted, a railroad in bad order may be likened to a common road full of holes and projecting stones; the best carriages will soon wear out on such roads; it is the same with cars on a railroad.

We will examine how a locomotive may produce injury, not speaking of wear and tear, on a railroad that is in good order; this is a very delicate question, and has always been a subject of controversy. Mr. Lechatelier has discovered that locomotives, as ordinarily constructed, acquire a serpentine motion, capable, within certain limits, of throwing the wheels off the rail. Having suspended a locomotive, with the fire kindled, in the air, the irregularity of its motions were studied, and a means was devised for putting the machine in equilibrium by the application of a counterweight to the driving wheels; this was found to neutralize these motions in a great measure. In this way the engine was kept steady upon the track, and found to do it less injury. This is the result of the researches of learned men, and it is generally understood and applied in France, and it will soon be in other countries. The use of the counterweight will be a powerful auxiliary in preventing the wear of the track and cars, and consequently will do away with motions so disagreeable to the passenger. Where the engines are not equilibriated, or where the track is out of surface or line, the engine drivers slacken for a time the speed of the train, if these motions become troublesome.

Besides these, there are other irregular motions of the train, names for which have been borrowed from the marine vocabulary; they are called the rolling and heaving of the engine; but these last motions never give rise to serious danger.

This instability upon roads where the line is straight may be remedied by a means of safety to which I would call the attention of companies; it is a close coupling of the trains, by which all the parts are consolidated. This mode is very rigidly practised in England, and the absence of it on other roads, particularly those of the south of Germany, seems inexplicable. The buffers being firmly pressed, and the cars brought close together, the whole train forms one mass, which is much more under the control of the engine driver than if the wagons had a play, and were confined merely by chains. This mode is generally adopted in France. It is found, in another form, upon American roads. Under each car an iron bar is fitted, pierced with a hole at its extremity; this is placed over the bar of the wagon behind it, and fitted by means of a bolt or pin passing through the two holes; this arrangement forms a single bar, flexible but not extensible. The shackling of cars is thus made more slow and difficult, but there is nothing to fear from rupture or shocks, and partial displacements from the rail, in changes of grade, or upon curves. In cases of collision the danger is diminished, since the shock is distributed through the whole mass, and the cars that are struck are less injured.

The aim of all constructors is to build cars whose regularity in running and whose stability shall be a security against danger.

In France and England, four-wheeled cars are preferred both for passengers and freight. Cars with six or eight wheels are rarely met with.

It is thought on many railroads, particularly in Germany, that four-wheel cars give rise to accidents, which are not recognized in England or France. No great importance is attached, in these two countries, to the advantages of six and eight-wheeled cars; advantages, that are much less striking than those of four wheels, which are more convenient in stations, and for crossing from one track to another, for the composition of trains, and especially for being placed on turntables, whose dimensions may be less if the shorter cars are used.

The superiority of cars with more than four wheels is theoretic rather than practical; those who advocate their use say that in forming trains, the number of cars, and, consequently, the intervals between them being less, the resistance of the air is diminished. To reduce, as much as possible, these intervals, the buffers on the road from London to Blackwall have been shortened, and they have been placed below the body of the car, so as to make the space between merely a few inches.

The stability of the car may be increased by increasing the distance between the axles, and does not depend altogether upon the number of wheels.

There has been but a single accident upon the Sceaux railroad, which has been in operation seven years. Does this depend upon the articulated cars, employed on this line by Mr. Arnoux, on the small amount of traffic, or on the wider guage, which is five feet and eleven inches instead of four feet eight and a half inches? This question is difficult to solve. But it can be affirmed with much certainty, that if this kind of car is employed upon important roads, accidents arising from running off the track will not be the same as those met with in rigid and independent cars.

Trials with these articulated cars are not sufficiently numerous to fix the precise limits of their use on inclines; as to the rate of speed on curves, it is not limited by the construction of these cars, but by the convenience of working the road, since the passengers cannot keep themselves in a vertical position while going round curves on a radius of eighty or a hundred feet; but they would be tossed about in a most disagreeable manner. To obviate this inconvenience, which may besides occasion accidents, the speed of the train should be slackened, and this is inadmissible on a road which requires a rapid and uniform rate of speed. It will be prudent then never to make use of curves of a less radius than three hundred and twenty-eight feet, and even to avoid the sudden passage from a tangent to a curve, by connecting the straight lines by arcs of parabolas; this is at least the advice of the commission, appointed by the Minister of Public Works, to examine into the modifications which the use of articulated cars will require in the working of roads already built, and the location of new ones. The report of this commission has been given to the public, and may be found in the Annales des Pont et Chaussees for March and April, 1853.

The present tendency is to make curves very sharp, and the trains very long. These two conditions can be united in the articulated cars alone, and on high rates of speed a greater stability is secured by them than by rigid trains.

CHAPTER X.

DEFECTS IN THE ROLLING STOCK.

There is still much room for improvement in the construction of railroad cars, both in reference to convenience and safety; and much attention is constantly devoted to this most important point. Open cars, cars without seats, cars with mere benches of wood, will soon disappear, and travellers will no longer be exposed to the inclemencies of the weather; they will no longer be crowded by fifties into cars with no means of support but bars and the walls of the car; they will soon all be comfortably seated, and will no longer reach the end of their journey worn out by fatigue. This is merely a question of cost.

Since the construction of railroad cars has been placed in the hands of carriage-makers, there has been great improvement in them, especially in France. It is not the same in other countries.

If the English cars are distinguished by ease of motion and stability, which arise from the good construction of the springs, the small size of the body, and close coupling; on the other hand they are wanting in elegance and convenience, and in this respect resemble those of Northern Germany.

Those convenient arrangements which are wanting in the passenger cars are found in those devoted to freight. The new freight cars have a roof of zinc or galvanized iron, which is kept in position by its own stiffness. Doors are cut in the sides, but more frequently there is an opening in the roof, through which goods are passed by means of cranes, which are found in sufficient numbers in their station grounds and buildings. Freight cars are almost always made of wood, but in some cases they are made of iron, especially those used for the transport of coke and coal. These iron cars are not likely to come into general use in France, on account of their great liability to be knocked out of shape.

Exotic woods, brought in great quantities from India as ballast, are exclusively used in the construction of English cars; the price of this wood is less than that of oak of the first quality. These woods are not painted, but simply polished; this would not be practicable in a country less cloudy than England.

With convenience and elegance we must combine in cars a strength equal to the shocks to which they are exposed. Light cars might be easily broken by these shocks, and the passengers thrown out; in cars excessively strong and massive, the occupants might be thrown about and wounded against the sides and salient angles scattered in profusion in the interior. The advice generally given to cover with cushions all projecting points is too little regarded. In many elegant cars, ornaments and carving, which interfere with a free circulation, are too often found.

In England the rolling stock is more substantially built than in France, and there, at present, the cars are not fitted to pass in succession over all lines, to be frequently lifted to considerable heights, and to remain for a long time absent from the places where they belong, and where alone they can be subjected to rigid examination and important repairs.

The only accidents that can happen to the bodies of cars are their destruction by fire or collisions. Accidents to cars are most frequently occasioned through faults in the axles, the wheels, and the mechanism for shackling. By the breaking of shackles, cars separated from the engine and abandoned to themselves have run down inclines, and have run into cars standing at stations, or coming in an opposite direction. The most careful inspection should be made of the bars for shackling and the safety-chains; for defects which have not been noticed and repaired in time, through the negligence or incapacity of the agent, have often occasioned accidents. On the railroad near Manchester, in 1852, a coupling-chain, which connected two locomotives to a train of fifty cars having broken, the engines went on alone, and having been very imprudently brought to a stop, the train ran into them with such violence as to break many cars in pieces and severely injure many passengers.

In locomotives, as in cars, the journals of the axles, or the oil-boxes, may get heated; this is made known by a grating sound, and the smell of burnt grease, or oil; the engine must be stopped, and water thrown upon them before they are oiled anew. If the connecting or piston rods, or the slides, become heated, they should be lubricated with all necessary precautions, and should be carefully looked to at every stopping place. Tightening in the cylinders arises from too great thickness of the covering of the segments of the piston. The cylinder head may be broken in consequence of the breaking of the pieces of the piston; the piston or connecting rod may break, and the pumps may refuse to work; in these cases, the engine must be stopped and put in order at once, or it may be ruined.

The parts which support the engine are also liable to accidents, which may cause the train to be injured or thrown off the track. The broken rods may fall down upon the track, raise up the engine and throw it off the track.

Springs, and tires too closely fitted may break, especially after long use, if proper care has not been taken in their manufacture; the flanges of the wheels may become loose; even if the pieces are not entirely broken, the train must be brought up at once by giving the usual signals.

The tender is not subject to any peculiar accident,

with the exception of the brake's getting out of order, and the precautionary measures to be taken are the same as those indicated for locomotives.

But of all the serious accidents to which the mechanism of a train is liable, the breaking of a locomotive axle may be placed in the first rank.

CHAPTER XI.

BREAKING OF AXLES.

An event happening in the month of May, 1842, on the railroad from Paris to Versailles, on the left bank of the river, caused by the breaking of an axle of the engine, fixed, very properly, the general attention on the construction of locomotives and the manufacture of axles; of which the form, strength, and durability leave little to desire at the present time. The breaking of them is becoming more and more rare in France. Nevertheless, we should not cease our attempts at improvement, nor wait till a fatal accident calls once more upon the skill of our workmen and inventors. The new axles are equal to all the exigencies of a sure and regular traffic. But will they always be so, or will they not become altered by prolonged use, as has already taken place upon many roads? What are the causes of this change, and by what signs can it be recognized? In regard to these questions there is great diversity of opinion.

These different opinions are based upon isolated experiments which have never been compared together, and which vary with different localities. This difference of opinion, as far as relates to modes of manufacture, is not of any great practical importance, and may depend upon different qualities in the iron. But it is of the greatest importance to settle what limits should be placed to the time which an axle may be safely used.

All the security and economy of working a railroad depends upon the solution of this question, At what time will it become necessary to renew the rolling stock and rails of roads? In France this question has not yet come up, though it has in some other countries.

The subject of the changes that take place in axles has been much discussed, and hypotheses, more or less plausible, have been imagined upon molecular movements and vibrations; on the other hand, a few experiments have been, and yet it was with them, that the beginning should have been made. Mr. de Boureuille, in a report presented in the name of the commission instituted in 1842, to discover the means of avoiding accidents on railroads, has considered this subject. His report, inserted in Les Annales des Ponts et Chaussees and the Annales des Mines, speaks of an apparatus for submitting axles of locomotives and cars to all the movements and resistances, to which they may be exposed in use. By this method, we shall evidently arrive at the same results as by observations of axles which have seen much service. This apparatus being kept in constant operation, enables us to arrive more speedily at an estimate of the course of crystallization, taking into account, at the same time, the changes occasioned in the nature of iron by variations of temperature.

The Austrian government has had the same idea, and it has the merit of having put it in operation some time since, in consequence of the almost daily breaking of axles, upon the State railroad, after having been kept in perfectly good order for five years.

I will give the experiments which have been made, and which I have before published in the Journal des Chemins de Fer, in answer to a wish expressed by the Society of Civil Engineers in Paris, that the limits of extensibility and compressibility of wrought iron might be subjected to special experiments.

The apparatus consisted of a bent axle, which was firmly fixed up to the elbow in timber, and which was subjected to torsion by means of a cog-wheel connected with the end of the horizontal part. At each turn the angle of torsion was 24°. A shock was produced each time that the bar left one tooth to be raised by the next. An index adapted to the apparatus indicated the number of revolutions and shocks. Seven axles, submitted to this trial, presented the following results.

1st. The movement lasted one hour: 10,800 revolutions and 32,400 shocks were produced. The axle, two and six tenths inches in diameter, was taken from the machine and broken by an hydraulic press. No change in the texture of the iron was visible.

2d. A new axle, having been tried four hours, sustained 129,000 torsions, and was afterwards broken by means of an hydraulic press. No alteration of the iron could be discovered, by the naked eye, on the surface of rupture; but tried with a microscope, the fibres appeared without adhesion, like a bundle of needles.

3d. A third axle was subjected, during twelve hours, to 388,000 torsions, and broken in two. A change in its texture, and an increased size in the grain of the iron, was observed by the naked eye.

4th. After one hundred and twenty hours, and 3,888,000 torsions, the axle was broken in many places; a considerable change in its texture was apparent, which was more striking towards the centre; the size of the grains diminished towards the extremities.

5th. An axle, submitted to 23,328,000 torsions during seven hundred and twenty hours, was completely changed in its texture; the fracture in the middle was crystalline, but not very scaly.

6th. After ten months, during which the axle was submitted to 78,732,000 torsions and shocks, fracture, produced by an hydraulic press, showed clearly an absolute transformation of the structure of the iron: the surface of rupture was scaly like pewter.

7th. Finally, as a last trial, an axle submitted to 128,304,000 torsions presented a surface of rupture like that in the preceding experiment. The crystals were perfectly well defined, the iron having lost every appearance of wrought iron.

From these experiments, we must conclude, that torsion and shocks exert a marked influence on the texture of iron, changing it from fibrous into crys-

5

talline iron. It is true that when an axle breaks, it suffers extraordinary torsions, for the rupture may be the consequence of the accident; a broken axle may throw the train off the track, and a train going off the track may produce the fracture of an axle. Straight axles break only in the journals,* crank axles may also break in the part forming the crank.

Let us examine now the irregular motions which bring about this alteration.

Shocks arise, firstly, from irregularities in the surface or line of the track, from the bending of rails, from the momentary depression of joints, from oscillations of the cars, and from the weight of the engine and the load pressing unequally upon the springs.

Torsions are produced by the unequal running of wheels with coned tires round curves; one of the wheels slides, while the other turns; this inequality of running of a cone on a plane surface is corrected by the torsion of the axle, which ceases, when its intensity, which corresponds to the elastic force of the iron, attains its maximum. Torsion takes place also upon straight lines, in consequence of the unequal diameter of the two wheels, of differences in the section of their tires, and in the inclinations of the rails, and finally by the distance between the axles. These evils may be remedied by a careful laying, and great convexity of the rail, for the flatter these are, the greater is the effect of sliding.

* American experience makes the fracture of axles occur, in a majority of cases, in the main part of the shaft, close to the inside face of the hub or nave. — *American Editor.*

The number of wheels has an influence on the torsion; it is desirable that experiments on this subject should be made with cars with four, six, and eight wheels. Practice alone can settle this question, which cannot be embraced, in all its particulars, by theory. The same process of crystallization is found going on in old structures of iron, either through the influence of heat, or of vibrations. The temperature of the air has a great influence on the condition of axles; during the first frosts, and after great thaws, the number of broken axles is apt to increase.

Almost all the inconveniences which have been spoken of, are, of necessity, incident to railroads, and it is impossible to do away with them altogether. The ingenuity of men is therefore directed to the manufacture of axles to resist all these evils. By suppressing the crank, which forms one plane of rupture, many accidents have already been avoided; and as regards the form, there is little room for improvement in axles. As to the mode of making, and the choice of material, there have been no innovations in France; in Germany, axles of steel have been used; in England, hollow, tubular axles have been tried, and upon two important roads, with apparent success; they have been applied to locomotives, where a high rate of speed is required under unfavorable circumstances. It is more in respect to superior powers of resistance, than in economy of iron, which is a quarter part less than that required for solid axles, that the hollow ones have the preference. Experiments which have been made to settle the merits of the two systems, *are in favor* of the hollow axles.

Nevertheless, all these trials are as yet too isolated, and experience has not settled the merits of the new methods so far as to lead us to advise a change.

In the mean time, great care should be used in the testing of axles; the most common method is to take, by chance, a certain number from a lot, and subject them to shocks till they are broken; from these the strength of the whole is inferred. This method is far from satisfactory; it is based upon a selection, more or less by chance, which can give only very uncertain results. As it is not prudent to employ a mode of testing, like that used for cannon, which may change the quality of the iron, a mode has been sought for which allows us to work directly upon the axle, without exceeding the limits of the elasticity of iron; the axles are loaded to this limit, and their powers of resistance are estimated according to the sines of flexion. The weakest axles are then broken and the grain of the metal examined.

The want of positive knowledge on this subject, shows the necessity of submitting this question to statistical investigation.

According to the royal ordinance of 1846, regulating the safety and the working of railroads, besides the general registers of locomotives, special registers are ordered to be kept, of all axles of locomotives, tenders, and cars, upon which, by the side of the number of each axle, shall be inscribed the place of its manufacture, the time it was put in use, the tests to which it has been subjected, its service, the accidents that have happened to, and the repairs which have been made upon it; a number corresponding to that of the register shall be punched upon each axle. These registers are to be presented, on demand, to the engineers and agents, charged with the examination of the material and working of the road.

Axles are subject to a second chance of accident; they may bend and throw the train off the track, especially while passing through frogs, in consequence of their irregular position in reference to the plane of the wheels; this causes an unequal wear in the flange, and consequently in the rail. The bending of axles may be occasioned by shocks arising from running too suddenly upon a switch and frog, by a load exceeding their limit of elasticity, and by an unequal wear of the tire.

It is necessary, in order to avoid keeping bent axles in use, to subject them to rigid examinations.

In consequence of the great liability of axles to become injured and broken, many plans have been proposed to prevent serious results from such accidents. All these plans may be referred to two general types. Guides suspended before the locomotive and over the rails, directing the engine till it is stopped. This supposes that a broken axle always throws the engine off the track, which is not the case. Besides, by this course the breaking of the axle is not discovered immediately. In the second place, beams armed with clogs, and fastened to the frame of the locomotive, lying along the line of the rail, have been proposed. The inconveniences which this invention would cause are greater than those it seeks to obviate. These clogs would break the track or break themselves, without keeping the engine in equilibrium; and if made strong enough to resist the shock they would be subjected to, would by their weight infallibly be the occasion of accidents.

Thus, at present, mechanical contrivances to insure safety to the train in cases of axles breaking, are wanting; we can depend only upon the skill of the engine driver, who by prompt and skilful management, when the engine begins to oscillate, may prevent serious results from the accident.*

In fine, to prevent breaking of axles, we should

1st. Perfect the process of manufacture.

2d. Experiment with steel and with hollow axles.

3d. Submit the question of the breaking of axles to a statistical investigation.

4th. Subject all axles to the test of bending, and to a daily inspection.

5th. Compare together the practical advantages of all inventions bearing on this question.

(In 1843, the fourth rule was prescribed by the Belgian Government.)

It may be thought that this discussion of axles has been carried to too great a length. For some time there has been no accident arising from the breaking

* A device termed safety beams, has been employed on American roads with great success. It is simply an iron suspension hook, fastened to the crosspiece of the truck, as close as practicable to the wheel, on the inside of it, in which the axle freely revolves. In case of fracture, the axle is sustained in its place and prevented from dropping down or flying up. Cars having this device, have been known to run safely many miles after fracture of the axle. — *American Editor.*

of an axle, but it seems to me that we should not wait till some serious accident awakens attention to this most important point.*

CHAPTER XII.

FAULTS IN THE RAIL.

Rails are subject, besides their unequal wear, to three chances of accidents, which may throw the train off the track; exfoliation, bending, breaking.

Exfoliation results from imperfections in the making, or from the rubbing of the rail by the wheel fixed by the brake; bending, from a disproportion between the size of the rail and the weight of the train; fracture is produced, when not the result of faults in the making, or atmospheric influences, by the shock from wheels whose tire has been unequally worn. The flange may strike upon the chair, raise the wheel, and cause it to fall upon the rail.

The breaking of rails is common, but upon straight lines it does not often produce serious accidents. It is most dangerous upon curves; and as the causes of it are, in some degree, beyond human knowledge, the means for preventing it cannot be completely pointed out.

In order to understand distinctly these accidents, we must know their origin, whether the fracture commenced with a fissure, which kept on increasing, per-

* See Appendix D.

haps for a long time, or whether it was caused by pressure merely, or by the shock of a wheel passing over a strange body, a super-elevation or bunch upon the rail. Before such an examination has been made, it will be very difficult to give an opinion on the subject; a minute examination into the causes of all breaking of rails upon all roads should be made. It may be shown, perhaps, that the shock of the wheel will only produce fracture in rails not permanently fixed in the chair; if this be so, it would be another argument in favor of rails permanently fixed.

The form of rails does not appear to exert a great influence in their deterioration, for one and the same form, employed upon one road, have remained uninjured by very heavy engines, while upon another, these rails have been broken by lighter locomotives doing the same amount of work.

There is no general rule upon this subject; the diversity in the forms of rails proves this. In this multitude of forms, six principal varieties may be distinguished.

1st. The double T used in France and England.

2d. The single T used in Belgium.

3d. The Brunel rail, U reversed, used in England.

4th. The American rail, with a single head, and large base, or Vignolles rail, T reversed, used in Germany.

5th. The Barlow rail, V reversed, which has been tried in England and in France.

6th. The compound, or Winslow's rail, which is split through the middle, and screwed together, used in America.

Experiments on rails have been made on a great scale upon roads in France. Barlow and Brunel's rail have been used; the last, at the time when other roads who have used it for ten years have discarded it. This shows an entire absence of method; a statistical investigation can alone indicate the proper course to be pursued, and we must by it determine the quality of all rails, and their effects in throwing trains off the track; not till then, can a decided opinion be given on this question, or can we see whether the shape of the rail has any influence upon this class of accidents. Such an investigation would determine the form of rail that gives the greatest security, and this would doubtless be immediately adopted upon all lines. In a problem so simple, as in all scientific questions, there can be but one solution; but science does not enable us to arrive at it *a priori.*

At the present time, however, the tendency is very evident, to give the head of the rail a very convex surface, to prevent the wheels wearing the edge of the rail, and producing exfoliation.

Besides, rails are now made with greater care, particularly since the methods of rolling have been improved to a degree that leaves little to be desired; and the manufacturers, being closely watched by the agents of the company, have a great interest in doing their work well. Those contracting for rails should see that the circular saw is not used in cutting them. This instrument works very quickly, but it has a serious evil of separating the fibres of the iron exactly at the point where it is of the last importance they should be most compact. In many shops the use of the saw has been abandoned and the rails are cut by the chisel; this process is slower, but it has the advantage of not altering the nature of the iron, and of diminishing in a great degree the quantity of refuse pieces.

Rails subjected to mechanical forces, are, at the same time, affected by atmospheric influences; they may break as a consequence of cold, or a high temperature may occasion irregularities in them.

The expansion of rails by heat, may cause them to spring out of line, so as to throw the train off the track. In 1842, on the St. Etienne road, a rail expanded by the heat was thrown ten feet out of line. This shows that the greatest care must be used in leaving the proper space at the joints while laying rails. On the same road, in 1844, some rails, being very much expanded, bent to such a degree that they raised themselves in the chair; the locomotive passing over them pressed down the first rail, and striking against the second was thrown off the track.

A broken rail may cause the wheels to strike against a chair and break it, and thus throw the train off the track.

Chairs not unfrequently break; this may be occasioned by imperfections in the casting, or by the flange striking them, from the tire being much worn. In these cases, as in the breaking of axles, counte rails do not seem to give any security; on the contrary, they increase the danger. It is true, they may arrest the tendency of the wheels to leave the rail, and may be used with advantage on very long viaducts, but they are of little use when the cars assume a serpentine motion, or when they have once left the rail. The wrong position of a counter rail threw a train off the track in 1846, at Irwell Bridge, on the Lancashire Railroad.

To prevent accidents as far as possible, great care must be taken in the superintendence of workshops, in the reception of rails, and the track must be very closely inspected at short intervals of time. These things are already done upon all well managed roads.

Before passing to an analysis of the use of signals, a part of which is trusted to the trackhands and watchmen, and an inattention to which is the most common cause of collisions, but a single accident remains to be spoken of, and that happily very rare, — burning of the cars.

CHAPTER XIII.

FIRES.

Fires caused by railroads were very frequent at an early stage of their history; they are now very rare, on account of the precautionary measures taken, and the improvements made in engines.

The covering of the boiler, which consists of felt and wood, to prevent cooling of the metal, may get on fire. An attentive engine driver perceives this at once, and drawing water from the tender puts it out; it has never caused serious results, and the consideration of it enters rather into the details of the management of the engine, than of accidents.

It is not so with fires which are caused on bridges, on the train, and on buildings situated along the line of the road, by sparks from the chimney of the locomotive, or by coals falling from the ash-pan. In 1847, Hanwell Bridge, on the Great Western Road, was burned down, by coals from the locomotive, and the travel was stopped. The transport of explosive substances upon railroads too often occasions explosions and fires; and a mode of preventing this class of accidents is well worthy the attention of inventors.

In order to put out the fire of the locomotive speedily, the bars of the grate have been made movable; these bars may fall upon the track and give rise to fires. Some contrivance may be devised to extinguish the fire in another way. A mechanism, consisting of a cock placed in the wall of the firebox so as to drown the fire is worth considering; it has not yet been brought into use. However, by the improvements introduced in the tops of the chimneys, and in ash-pans, these accidents are becoming of less importance every day. Some years ago, fears upon this subject were very great. The use of locomotives was forbidden, on considerations of public safety, on a road passing through a portion of London, and the cars were moved by a cable worked by a stationary engine. Experience has shown the needlessness of this precaution, and the locomotives are again used.

Among the exceptional accidents occasioned by

fire may be cited the explosion of a quantity of powder carelessly placed in a freight train on the Glasgow road in 1850; the destruction of a part of the Birmingham viaduct, by the explosion of illuminating gas, which had infiltrated into a cavity of the masonry from a leak in the gas pipe placed along this viaduct; the gas was set on fire by contact with a heated part of the locomotive, at least this is the opinion of the commissioners given in their official report. These extraordinary facts are only given to prove the utility of the most minute precautions and the closest attention to the details of working a road.

Fires sometimes arise from the carelessness of passengers. I lately saw an English family preparing breakfast by means of a lamp of spirits of wine placed on a table in the saloon of a car. On the starting of the train, the least shock might have upset this impromptu kitchen, and given rise to serious injury. Such offences need only be pointed out to be done away with; and I think the simplest way in such cases, to guard against the carelessness of fellow-travellers, is to speak at once to the conductor.

CHAPTER XIV.

INATTENTION TO SIGNALS.

There is no general rule to be pointed out with regard to signals. The use of them belongs to all branches of the working department, and should be understood by all persons engaged upon the track or the train.

Signals may be divided into three classes: —

Acoustic and movable signals, given directly by the *employés*, — the flag, lantern, the sound of a horn or whistle.

Fixed signals, moved by mechanism, dials, reflectors, torpedoes, optical or aerian telegraphs.

Lastly, the electric telegraph.

All these signals are good, when they are well observed; when they can be verified and understood. The difficulty in their use, in all possible cases, calls forth the study of the engineer: what can be done, when the lanterns go out, during thick fogs, falls of snow, breaking of the telegraph wires, is a doubtful question. This question is properly considered in a treatise on the working of roads. Signals are most complicated, and play the most important part upon single track roads, being, as it were, the base of the service; and as they are not infallible, as they must be perceived and understood at once, the question has often been raised, whether single track roads present more chances of accident than double track ones. This question has never been absolutely settled, for theory does not admit of collisions. Statistics should point out the way to a solution; this it has not as yet done, for the results furnished by this modern science are contradictory. In the kingdom of Wurtemberg, there has never been a collision, and the roads are all single track; in the Grand Duchy of Baden, there has been but one, since the opening in 1840, and that was at the entrance of a side track, in the very place where the track was double. I am far from attempting to settle this question; for opposite opinions are maintained by competent men.

Infallible signals, as well as means for stopping a train instantly when signals have been disregarded, to prevent collisions and running off the track, have occupied the minds of inventors. In attempting to diminish the injury caused by these accidents, inventors admit that they are, like an inevitable fatality, an integral part of the working of a road; and they endeavor to find means for preserving the passengers, sometimes by *parachocs* and machines with compressed air to operate on the brakes; spectacles of a peculiar form have even been invented to enable the engine driver to see at a great distance the train coming to meet him. The engine driver is thus changed into a watchman, as though trains were destined to run into each other, and as though spectacles could be of any use in the night, in dense fogs, and on curves; in a word, in all cases where there could be any chance of collision, these spectacles could be of no use.

I will say no more on this subject, not wishing to

object by sterile criticism to the application of these discoveries, which often have one useful side; they denote a praiseworthy desire on the part of their authors to make themselves useful to their fellow men, and on this account, are entitled to our respect; but it is to be desired, that these efforts should be directed to the more practical object of improving engines, modes of laying rails, crossings, signals of correspondence between those on the train in case of the breaking of a coupling iron or a tire, in a word, all the details indispensable to regularity of service, many of which, now in use in other countries, are unknown on French roads.

It is only by centralizing all these inventions and submitting them to direct trial, that useful results can be obtained.

We read in the United States Journal, that a society of inventors has been formed in New York, under the name of "The American and Foreign Patent Agency Company." Its object is the introduction and sale of patent rights, and things patented, as well as to watch over the interests of inventors. The office of this company, the Pantheon of New York, will be a central point for all America; new inventions will be exhibited there; agencies will be established in the different cities of the United States; and all inventions will be submitted to a committee, called the Board of Examiners, who will make reports upon the value of the inventions.

CHAPTER XV.

COLLISIONS.

It is well known, that the public is soon accustomed to high rates of speed, when they can be obtained without danger. In this respect, the English have always held the first rank, both upon the water and upon common roads. The same is true upon railroads, their express trains going regularly at the rate of forty-eight miles an hour. This limit has not been reached in France; the other continental roads are limited to half that speed. It is only till very lately that express trains at high rates of speed have been organized on the continent.

Much attention should be fixed on the measures to regulate this service and to guard against the chances of collision.

This accident occurs when two trains, going in different directions, meet; when one following another overtakes it, and when a train coming in, runs into another standing at a station. These three kinds of accidents form a very distinct classification.

In the first case, the accident arises from a non-observance of the time and rules of starting, or from an extra engine injudiciously directed.

The second case happens through irregularities in running the trains.

The third, from the engine driver not having given,

in time, the signal for using the brakes, and not having closed the regulator soon enough.

In the first case, the engine driver having the right to the track, cannot expect to be met; the shock is inevitable, for the signals cannot be given in time; on a straight line, however, of any great length, there is no danger if proper precautions are used.

The observance of the times for starting regular trains, is then an essential condition of safety, especially upon single track roads. Inattention to this rule, simple as it is, occasioned twenty-three collisions upon English roads in the year 1851; the jury of inquest settles this fact, and the report of the commissioners relates it. It is even astonishing that there were not more accidents, for coal and freight trains are often sent out under the charge of an engine driver, whose only instructions are to take up or leave cars on the route, and to arrive as quick as possible at his place of destination; his course is regulated by telegraphic announcement, and by the order to keep a certain interval between two trains, and to place his train on the side track, when the express or passenger trains are signalized. Every thing depends upon signals, and a single one wrongly given is almost sure to bring about an accident.

This mode of proceeding is often the rule in England; on the continent it is an exception.

When from the exigencies of the service, extra trains or single engines are needed, the greatest care must be used lest they run into the regular trains.

On double track roads, all the trains keeping the left track, there is no chance of trains meeting; this can only occur while repairs are going on upon one of the tracks. The road should then be managed as a single track road, and the modes of regulating trains suited to such a road, applied to it. It is mainly upon these roads, of which I shall soon speak, that the running of extra trains presents real dangers.

Extra engines may be injudiciously directed when demands for help are sent, from a disabled train, to two stations at once, and when the train starts as one of the assisting engines is on the point of arrival. In these circumstances, every thing depends upon the intelligence and vigilance of those in charge of the train. Engines may start by themselves, and break, in their blind course, every thing that is found on the track. After a time they stop, and, if suitable signals are given, they may be brought without accident into the depot. No analysis of facts enables me to determine the causes of these sudden starts.

In the second case, it may happen, in consequence of differing rates of speed, one train may run into another; the greater part of the accidents on English roads are of this nature. In clear weather, and when the trains carry lights, this accident cannot occur except through unpardonable negligence of the agents of the company; but it is not so, in the thick fogs, so common in England, and in such cases the absence of immediate watchfulness is sensibly felt. For cases of this kind, many measures have been proposed; signals indicating the passage of trains have been placed along the line, and by means of explosive signals, points of danger are made known to the engine driver. Two trains cannot run together in this way, except where the signals for delaying or stopping the trains have been badly given, or misunderstood. To avoid this accident, the greatest possible interval must be left between two trains; the amount of this interval depends upon the speed of the trains, the grades, the power of the brakes, and a mass of details too great to be enumerated.

To settle this distance, which in many countries has been fixed in an arbitrary and general manner, we must look at the matter in the most unfavorable light; in the night, in thick fogs, at the highest rate of speed, and calculate at what point a signal should be placed, to be understood by those on the train following, in order that they may stop it by applying the brakes; when this distance is once found, it should be used in an absolute manner by all trains under all circumstances.

Here is a fact which supports what I have just said; it is taken from a journal called L'Emancipation Belge.

An accident, which might have had the most disastrous consequences, happened in the month of October, at the station at Hall. The eight and a half o'clock train stopped to unload and take up some cars, when suddenly the signal of a freight train, which had been concealed by the fog, was heard. It was impossible to get the train off the track, for most of the cars were unshackled; it was equally impossible to stop the coming train, for it was very near, and coming at a high rate of speed. The switchman ran to the front to warn the engine driver; in the mean time, the depot master had warned the passengers of the coming danger. These, mostly shoemakers of Hall, who went every week to Brussels with their goods, took but little time to say goodby. In a moment, bootmakers, buskins, and boots were all in the ditch. The last passenger had scarcely quitted the train, when the collision took place. The last car, which was a diligence, was literally pulverized, the others were proportionally damaged. But fortunately, in neither train was any passenger injured; a moment sooner, and the victims would have been numerous. This system of allowing trains to follow each other at too short intervals should be altogether condemned, for at the slightest accident on a curve, or in a fog, a heavy loaded freight train not being brought up in time by the brakes, may run into the train which has preceded it.

In the third place; in order that the trains may not enter the side tracks at too high a speed, it has been advised, that the conductor should leave the train and walk by its side, for the brakes may be out of order, and may not work readily at the first sound of the whistle. This course may give rise to accidents, as the chief engineer of the line of the Grand Duchy of Baden writes me, but I think it should be followed, especially upon single track roads, on account of an accident which happened some years since, where a train on a side track being just about to start, was run into by a train coming in.

Where this precaution is not used, and unfortunately too frequently, trains run into each other at stations. The electric telegraph, enables us to guard against these dangers; it is therefore very generally used; on many of the main lines, there are fifteen wires, for the use of the public and the railroad.

The signals for the day are given at the stations, or at the points of connection with branch roads, by a switchman placed upon a platform, giving a fair view of the trains as they arrive and depart. This post is very important, especially at times, when the locomotive is detached from the cars, to run into the engine house, while the cars follow the main track by their acquired velocity.

Brakes are the only means at present used, for slackening the speed of trains. In spite of the defects inherent in this system, energetic brakes have been of great service, and have often prevented serious accidents; without the Laignel Brake, which rests upon the rail, and raises the car, the Royal Belgian train could not have escaped a terrible catastrophe, when the cable of the inclined plane at Liege broke. Modes of stopping trains are constantly being investigated, and there is no want of inventions to secure this end.

The study of powerful brakes is by no means exhausted, and machinists have constantly endeavored to perfect them; a brake roughened and resting on the rail or even on the road-bed, a sort of brake *de misericorde*, may often be of undoubted use. From the want of such a brake, on the Wurtemburg roads, a barrier of strong oak beams has been placed across the track, at the foot of steep inclines, suited to stop cars whose brakes do not work with effect. In 1849, some empty cars, going down this plane, acquired a velocity beyond control; those upon them leaped to the ground, and abandoned them to their fate; they were broken against this barrier within a few feet of a train standing at the station.

The English commissioners, in their annual report, attribute the frequent collisions to the want of effective brakes, especially when the rails have become polished, as they must be after long service.

For some time past, a new kind of brake, similar to the shoe used for common carriages, has been made use of in England. Instead of acting by means of a pressure applied directly to the wheel, this shoe is placed between the rail and the tire of the wheel; it is flat below and concave above; it is dropped before the wheel, which runs upon it, and presses it with all its weight upon the rail. This improvement, which is also a simplification, presents many advantages; the shoe produces great friction upon the rail, whilst with the common brake, the pressure is exerted upon the tire of the wheels, which slide over the rails, and are therefore very rapidly worn; the shoe is made of the proper thickness, to guard against the flange of the wheel riding over the rail, and thus throwing the car or engine off the track. To free the brake, the train should be backed a little.

The design of this shoe brake is old; Mr. Laignel having taken out a patent for it on the twenty-eighth of February, 1841.

CHAPTER XVI.

IRREGULARITY IN THE RUNNING OF TRAINS.

Admitting, for a time, the accidents which frequently happen to trains and locomotives running out of time, without being properly signalized, we must explain how it happens, that the times of arrival and departure are not strictly adhered to.

The causes of delay are of four kinds: —

1st. The want of exactness in the times of starting, stopping, and arriving; this is remedied by a revision of the calculations, and suiting the time to the exigencies of the traffic; this cause need only exist at the commencement of the working of the road.

2d. Want of power in the locomotive, when the train is too heavily loaded, when the pressure of steam has not been well kept up, or when the rails have become slippery from rains, frost, or thick fogs; the wheels have not then a sufficient hold on the rails, and the engine moves slowly. The general remedy for this evil is very simple, we must merely make the maximum load equal to the minimum power of the engine; or in other words, find out the load the engine can draw under the most unfavorable circumstances; in winter, in a storm, on the heaviest grades, at the highest rates of speed.

To get at these results each engine must be submitted to experiments and calculations, upon a given plane, with fixed conditions, in order to discover its power. This being fixed, will serve as a basis in the composition of trains, and should be inscribed on the engine, as the load is upon cars.

The want of exact calculation in this respect occasions accidents. In 1851, on a branch of the road from Manchester to Chester, two extra trains having started at short intervals were obliged to stop in a tunnel. The first engine could not draw its load over the grade, and the second engine was not powerful enough to push it; a third train came into the tunnel, and not having been noticed by the trains there, ran into them and killed many persons.

The third cause of delay, may be the occurrence of any accident whatever. The train is then stopped until the damage is repaired. If this delay requires that the coming train shall be met at some point other than the usual one, no precaution should be neglected, and arrangements should be made for such cases, by the superintendent; orders to start should be given in writing, unless the electric telegraph gives assurance that every thing is right: where this is used the question and answer should be given three times, before the train is allowed to start. The passage of extra trains should be signalized over the whole route.

Finally, the way may be obstructed by foreign bodies upon it, as slides of earth, forgotten tools, etc. Those employed on the train can clear the track, and the lost time is often regained.

There is a kind of obstruction capable of retarding the trains in a sensible manner, and often of stopping them indefinitely, namely, snow, on which point it may be useful to enter into some details, and to the examination of which I shall devote a chapter.

CHAPTER XVII.

INTERRUPTION OF COMMUNICATION BY SNOW.

As we have seen, the working of trains may be interrupted by injury to the engine, or accidents to the cars or the track; but with the exception of the fall of a piece of masonry or a bridge, communication is soon renewed, except in cases where snow produces such an obstruction as cannot be speedily removed by the means ordinarily in use.

This is the weak point of railroads, which, in winter, are far from giving to passengers the security and convenience desired.

The attempt to work a line with regularity during the winter season has not been given up; but on the other hand, the problem has not been solved in a general manner. Despairing of effecting this object, with effective machines, some engineers have proposed to organize a special service during snowstorms, as we have already trains for summer, and trains for winter, which should consist of a small train of cars with two locomotives ahead. The consideration of this is not out of season; for this mode of working trains is not only feasible upon all roads, but is already in practice on some at very difficult points, and I think that after a close study of all the circumstances connected with it, we shall no longer, in France, be exposed to the delays, interruptions, and accidents, which are a natural, if not an inevitable consequence of all changes in the regular running of trains.

To point out the causes of these obstructions by snow, as well as the means to be employed to prevent accidents in consequence of them, as well to the trains as the telegraphic wires, I must enter into some developments and explanations of meteorologic phenomena. I shall thus indicate the starting point of an investigation which will sooner or later be entered upon to secure the safety of the public.

Accumulations of snow depend upon the nature of the snow, the force and direction of the wind, and the climate and topographical position of the places exposed.

There are two kinds of snow, considered with reference to the present subject: moist snow, which on account of the adhesive property of its particles, is not easily driven about by the wind; this is not dangerous; dry or powdery snow, which is driven about by the least breath of wind, and raised up, when the wind is strong, in whirlwinds, and deposited in large masses, as the wind subsides; the snow swept from the heights being left in the valleys.

Numerous observations on this subject have been made on the railroads of the north of Germany. They can be classified as follows:

1st. Railroads are not liable to be blocked up by

snow in cuts, when they are surrounded by forests, or when the centre line lies in the same direction with the course of the wind.

2d. Trees and hedges planted along the track, break the violence of the wind, and compel the snow to fall in a vertical line.

3d. Winds, blowing in the direction of the line of the railroad, clear it of snow.

4th. If the railroad, located in the open country, or on high land, crosses the line of the storm, the snow will become heaped up in light cuts; in heavy cuts, on the contrary, the snow accumulates upon the top of the slopes; the force of the wind is broken in the cuts, and the snow falls quietly and uniformly, as in the forests.

5th. The most favorable condition, when the road crosses the line of the storm, is that where the rails are on a level with the natural surface of the ground; the wind sweeps uninterruptedly over the track, which is then covered like the adjoining country.

6th. Heavy embankments present the inconvenience, that the wind, sweeping over the country, breaks on their crest, forms whirlwinds on the track, and deposits the snow on the rails.

7th. In all cases, embankments are less likely to be filled up with snow than the cuts.

8th. The dangerous dry snows are brought by winds from the north and west, and are always accompanied by the most severe cold.

These indications may form the basis of investigations for the location of railroads, for constructions to be added to roads already built, and for the arrangement of machines to clear off the snow from the track.

There has been no attempt as yet to locate a road so as to protect it from snow; the liability to obstruction from this cause being admitted, means have been adopted to protect the line from the snow-bearing winds. Hedges and fences of pine boards, about six feet high, have been placed along the most exposed portions of the line. Embankments have even been thrown up for the same purpose.

All these means have been employed on the Bavarian Railroad, from the Lake of Constance to Hof, in that portion which includes the heavy grades of one hundred and thirty-two feet to the mile, for a distance of three and one tenth miles. During a most snowy winter, in 1850, the communication was not interrupted for a single day. On twenty-seven points fences have been placed to break off the snow: seventeen against the west wind; six against the east wind, four against the southeast wind.

The effect of these snows is often very surprising; depending upon the direction of the valleys, the forests, and the position of the villages. Often points, whose position, at first sight, seems most unfavorable are spared; while others, which do not seem particularly exposed, are covered by the first snows.

There is no general rule applicable to these cases. By a long and careful study of the meteorologic phenomena, in any particular locality, we may discover indications for the location of embankments, the placing of fences, and the planting of trees or hedges. The protection of railroads from snow is a practical matter; and what I have said on this subject should be merely considered as hints for further investigation. The best thing to be done, if we wish our trains to run in France with regularity during the winter, would be to send a commission to other countries, to study this question, and to make a practical examination of it during at least one winter. They would be able to inform themselves, at the same time, in respect to all new arrangements for clearing the track of snow, and in due time make them useful. The means commonly used in France, are the snow plough, and brooms attached to the locomotive and cars. These means are very feeble, and for the most part without effect. Then there are bodies of workmen, suddenly called together to shovel out the snow; to remove the obstruction, where perhaps, it might have been prevented by an expenditure of a less amount of money. In 1854, the Paris and Strasbourg Railroad paid nearly $18,000 for the removal of a million cubic yards of snow. All these modes will be improved, for the genius of inventors is directed to this end. A machine will be some day invented for this purpose, which will take the place of the locomotive, which expending all its force to overcome the snow and wind has none left with which to draw the train. As its speed is slackened by the work, less steam is generated; it can no longer rise over the heavy grades, where the snow hardened by the pressure of cars and by the frost, resists the wheels like wedges placed upon the rail; it is stopped also on rails, where the workmen passing over have left lumps of snow which have been hardened into ice.

Beside the accidents caused by delays in the starting and arrival of trains, by a relaxation in strictness on the part of the watchmen, by engines going over the line in search of disabled trains, which may come when they are least expected; in a word, beside all these inevitable irregularities, it almost always happens, to increase the difficulties, that the electric telegraph fails to work, either from the wires breaking, or from their touching each other. In 1849, on the South-eastern road, many telegraph posts were thrown down; every running foot of the wire, with its coating of ice, weighed nearly four pounds; so that the post was subjected to the weight of thirty-three hundred pounds. Many of the iron wires were bent to the ground, but when the weight was taken off, they resumed their original positions; while the copper wires having lost all their elasticity remained bent. In 1850, on the Northern road, in Austria, the upper wire, being heavily loaded, touched the lower one, so that the electric current was absorbed, and no messages could be transmitted.

As the bending and breaking of the wires occur very often from this cause, the watchmen should shake the posts, so that the snow may fall while it is yet soft; by this simple precaution, these accidents may always be prevented. It is also well to take off from the posts the coatings of ice which would, if permitted to touch the isolators, discharge the electric current. All this is well known; but it is desirable that it should be more noticed and more carefully attended to.

CHAPTER XVIII.

DIFFICULTIES OF WORKING A SINGLE TRACK ROAD.

The main difference between double and single track roads as regards accidents, consists in the liability to collisions between trains running in opposite directions. The most simple rule to avoid these, and one which presents itself to every mind, is for no train to start, till the one expected has arrived. How is it, that this rule is not always observed? Why is any reliance placed upon a supposed certainty that the track is clear? Why is a train allowed to start out of its regular time? Why, in fine, are trains exposed to such terrible consequences, by neglect of these rules? These are questions little understood, and the solution of which is unknown to the public; negligence on the part of the *employés* is not suspected, and inattention to the rules of the service and the signals seems inexplicable.

I will endeavor to answer in detail these questions; but before doing so, I will relate a fact bearing on this subject, which is always present to my memory, though it happened more than twelve years ago. It includes all the causes and chances of collisions, and shows a mode of avoiding them, without causing too great irregularity in working the trains.

In the Grand Duchy of Hesse, on a road with a single track, as almost all the German roads are at the present time, I found myself in the cars, waiting on the side track for the arrival of another train. At this time the common signals were used, the electric telegraph not having come into general use. Through these signals, a despatch arrived, announcing that in consequence of an accident to the locomotive, the expected train would not leave the station. The depot master gave the order to start, and attempt to regain the lost time; the engine driver made no reply, but examined the safety-valves to see that they worked well, slackened the fire, and sitting quietly down, with the fireman, said that the superintendent had directed him always to wait for a train that was coming in the opposite direction. The depot master, strong in his authority, and the certainty that the delayed train would not come, repeated his order; the engine driver replied that it was useless to go on; that sooner or later the other train would arrive if the track was passable. The passengers were not of his opinion; they joined in the discussion, which soon became very animated, and the *gendarmes* finally took the men from the engine. Night had come on. A new engine driver was found; the signal for starting was given; all the passengers had got into the cars, and the bell had just stopped ringing, when a prolonged whistle was heard in the distance, and the delayed train came along under a full head of steam.

Here are the answers to the questions proposed.

Trains are not kept waiting for fear of disturbing the service; reliance is placed on the tracks being clear, because it is hoped, that he who has given the notice of a clear track, will not send a train or an engine upon it within a fixed time; trains are started out of time, so that the passengers, in case of any delay, need not have to wait until the next train, which with a single engine, may not be able to haul two trains ; for often the use of two engines together is not allowed by the rules of the road; and as trains are not allowed to follow each other at short intervals, extra locomotives have to be sent to succor disabled trains: in fine, accidents arise from inattention to rules, because the execution of these, however precise they may be, are intrusted to men, who are far from perfect, who do not always feel the importance of their duties, and who are dissatisfied with their work.

But, in spite of all these imperfections, are there any efficacious means to prevent accidents upon a long single track road, and at the same time, keep up the activity of the traffic and regularity in the running of the trains?

Many means of safety have been presented; it is especially after a serious accident that inventions arise, as if the human mind had always need of a stimulus to impel it to a search for its well-being. We have already examined these inventions, and those applicable to single track roads with the rest.

In roads of this description every thing depends upon mathematical regularity in the running of the trains. There are no general rules to be laid down on this subject.

In single track roads, the running of the trains, and the points where trains should take the side track for others to pass them, should be fixed in the most exact manner. It would be prudent to restrain the use of extra trains within very narrow limits. Nevertheless, if in consequence of an accumulation of freight, extra trains become indispensable, they should be placed upon the time table, a copy of which should be given to every conductor; these trains then become regular trains; and even when it is found that one of them is not absolutely needed, it is better that it should be continued, even at some little expense, than to cause irregularities in the working of the road, which always happen when the hours of starting are changed. Above all things regularity in the hours of starting should be maintained, and nothing should be spared to secure it.

Special arrangements are sometimes necessary; as the measure taken to make collisions impossible in the tunnel, three miles long, on the road from Manchester to Sheffield; here each train is hauled through by a locomotive specially devoted to this purpose. As the grade falls in each direction from the centre of the tunnel, the second engine serves as an accessory to help the other over the grade.

Arrangements like this are not always applicable. The basis of service of single track roads is the use of side tracks for the passing of trains; without these, the least delay in any train whatever, will be felt over the whole line; and the service will be suspended on the whole road, until the travel is resumed on the part affected. At first, proper prudence was not exercised in this matter, and accidents occurred. Had these increased, we should have been compelled to renounce the use of side tracks, and seek another mode of working out of the difficulty, namely to back the trains.

Fortunately it is not so, and accidents upon lines that have long been open, have been less and less frequent, in proportion as those employed have acquired the necessary knowledge, and mechanical contrivances have been perfected; besides, the traffic does not sensibly increase upon single track roads, for when it is developed to a great degree, another line of rails is laid, and it becomes a double track road.

The best thing to be done, if we would make use on a large scale of this kind of road in France, would be to investigate on the roads themselves every thing that cannot be otherwise learned. In my opinion this is the only way; it is not that we cannot get accounts of the best mode of working single track roads, or that the most perfect mechanism, or the strictest rules are wanting; for in spite of the multitude of precautions taken, the desired result is not reached. We must look into this matter more deeply; facts prove it. What we want is men to apply all the rules that have been laid down, and to familiarize themselves with the modes of working which have been practised since these roads began to be worked. We must know for what objects German engineers have gone to America, and why we have sent for English ones to come here. The organization of the service, the position of the different agents, their character, their antecedents, the manner in which rewards and promotions, fines and punishments are administered, and in fine, the effects of the whole course of discipline practised upon roads of this description must be investigated. We should study the relations between superintendents and those employed by them, and follow out the mechanical arrangements from their inception to their perfection; in a word, we must serve an apprenticeship in this practical science, and discover the modifications made necessary by the habits, exigencies, and character of the French public.

This is very difficult, very laborious, and very costly; but it is also very difficult to work a single track railroad, without having any accident to deplore, and this point we have not as yet reached.

I do not think that either England or the United States will give us better examples, than Germany, where single track roads have been operated on a great scale, with a large amount of travel and with trains at a high rate of speed. In that country, accidents due to the single track system are very rare, and only happen at the stations, where the trains run into each other, in consequence of not properly slackening up, or from the switches being set wrong.

In France, these facts are not considered, for the operations on the single track road of Orleans have, whether justly or not, thrown discredit upon this class of roads, which may continue for some time. The public thinks little of financial or technical details: it demands, above all things, security in a system of conveyance, which has the monopoly of all rapid travel. Besides, up to the present time, we have not given sufficient attention to the single track, for with the exception of the Sceaux and the Troyes roads, it has never been regularly established with us, as in Germany.

In fine, the mode of working a single track road cannot be studied in books, or even by conversation with men most versed in the matter. I repeat it, if we wish to introduce this system into France, we must send agents of every rank and grade, from our companies, to learn the trade upon roads already in operation, and they must there study men as well as things.

" The rarity of accidents on our railroads," the director-general of railroads of the Kingdom of Wurtemburg writes me, " is owing not to any superior knowledge, but to the punctuality and regularity of the service. We employ no other signals than those indicated in the signal book, commonly used by engine drivers and watchmen. The electric telegraph, whose stations are on an average seven miles apart, serves for the transmission of messages and government orders as well as for public use. In exceptional cases the correspondence of the railroad administration is transmitted before private despatches."

We see, by this, that in working a road, practice is worth more than any kind of theory or dissertation; at least, such is my opinion.

CHAPTER XIX.

IMPRUDENCE OF PERSONS TRAVELLING OR EMPLOYED ON THE TRAIN.

ACCIDENTS caused by the fault of passengers or those employed on the train were very numerous at the time when people had not become accustomed to this mode of travelling. These often happened from attempts to get off or on the train while in motion. It was soon found out that such attempts almost always occasioned severe wounds or death. One must be very adroit to jump off a car travelling at a high rate of speed, and the platform must be pushed by the foot in the direction the train is going in order to deaden the shock. But this is always dangerous, and can never be practised with any chance of success, except by those accustomed to it; it may be done by those employed on the train, in case of danger, when their presence is of no more use, when the whistle has been sounded, the brakes put on, and the steam reversed.

Accidents owing to the carelessness of travellers, and persons not connected with the road, cannot be considered in a treatise of this nature. What preventive means can be devised for persons who walk carelessly upon the track; for those who sleep on the rails; who jump from the cars, and are crushed by the train; who let things fall upon the track, as happened on an English road near Hull, where a bit of iron falling from a car threw a train off the track, and cost the lives of five persons? How can we prevent people from raising themselves up on the seats of *Imperials* at the entrance of tunnels? from putting out their heads while passing through bridges, or entering depots? How can we secure workmen from being injured in making up trains, or from falling into ditches? Many such accidents are caused by the carelessness of those injured, as is shown by statistics.

Those employed on the road may also be guilty of acts of carelessness which endanger the passengers. They may leave cars at stations where they ought not to be left, they may forget their tools, or leave an engine standing on the track, or take up rails, when a train is due. Here are some examples which I have taken from foreign roads.

It is well known how dangerous it is to run a locomotive with the tender in front, and many examples prove this. A beam inadvertently placed on the rails of a branch of the Brighton road threw a train off the track in the month of June, 1851: the tender in this case was in front. The English jury, called to decide upon the cause of the death of six persons killed by this accident, asked for a law forbidding all engines running with the tender in front, unless furnished with means for clearing obstructions from the track.

A special train had carried the King of Belgium to Ostend in 1838, and returned at night. The bridge of Sneppe, was unfortunately open; the locomotive cleared the opening, but held by the weight of the cars which fell into the river, it was drawn back upon and crushed them; two persons were killed, and another severely wounded.

A close watch should be kept over cattle in the neighborhood of roads, and over those transported over them. Accidents very frequently happen from want of this watchfulness, especially in America, where they have even invented arrangements for the purpose of throwing cattle off the track. A horse getting away from his owner fell upon the track, and threw off a train; this accident happened on the Hamburg road.

The least forgetfulness or the slightest negligence may produce the most serious consequences.

In the month of July, 1845, a train left London for Dover drawn by two locomotives. At one of the way stations it was discovered that the lantern of the last car had been left behind: this not having been discovered till the train had started, a locomotive was sent on with it, which came upon the train with such force at the entrance of a tunnel, as to break up many cars filled with passengers. It is well known that trains should never be pushed by the engine, or if the exigencies of the service require it, that it should be done with the greatest caution. But unfortunately attention is not always paid to this elementary rule; for in 1847, a train of forty cars was pushed up an incline on the Great Western road; a coupling chain breaking, caught in the point of a frog, and threw a part of the train off the track.

Without perceiving the accident, the engine driver pushed on the cars, which were crushed with all that they contained; fortunately they were nothing but cattle.

The enumeration of all these facts would constitute the true statistics of accidents. To prevent carelessness on the part of *employés*, we can only recommend to agents to attend carefully to the character of those they employ; they may thus form a body of men, always attentive, and ready to obey.

In order to guard as much as possible against accidents to the train, during the journey, means have been devised to put the conductor in communication with the engine driver. Many means have been proposed and in part applied for this end; the want of them has already been the cause of many accidents; and especially in cases of fire these means of communication might be of the greatest use.

CHAPTER XX.

WANT OF COMMUNICATION BETWEEN THE CONDUCTOR AND THE ENGINE DRIVER.

The establishment of a direct communication between the guards of the cars, the travellers, and the engine driver, has for a long time occupied the attention of those connected with railroads; but this question has never been settled in a positive manner.

The delegates of the *Railway Clearing House*, have submitted it to an examination very much in detail; they are surrounded with the means necessary to test the advantages of all the systems that have been used or designed, but they have rejected one after the other.

Metallic rods fixed on the roof of the cars, enabling the conductor to act on the steam whistle, appear to them, to present difficulties in adjustment, and to expose the workmen to danger in coupling the cars.

Tubes of gutta percha, joined together by india-rubber, with whistles connected with lateral tubes for the passengers, and establishing a communication between the engine driver and those on the train, do not appear to answer. In a trial made with a tube three hundred and ninety-four feet long, the sound was transmitted very distinctly, but the words could not be understood; and besides, the opportunity of giving the signal to stop and of communicating with the engine driver, should not be given to the passenger, as in the opinion of the delegates, it would be likely to give rise to accidents.

The whistle of compressed air does not appear to be strong enough in some cases; the steam whistle, even the strongest, cannot always be heard at the end of the train.

Portable electric telegraphs, as well as electric chimes appear to be too delicate, and on that account of doubtful effect.

Platforms placed along the cars, upon which the conductors can readily pass, or the American cars with a passage way through the centre, could not be used in England, being contrary to the character and habits of the English people.

In general, optical means appear insufficient, especially in the night and in tunnels, and they are of no use in fogs. The ordinary acoustic means are inapplicable in high winds or at rapid rates of speed. Communications by means of elastic cords present difficulties in consequence of the great difference in the size of the cars, and the complications caused by the arrangements of trains, the composition of which varies at almost every station; these cords might also be caught between the cars.

In fine, none of these arrangements seem to the committee proper to be applied in England, and it proposes to companies, as a means of communication, to place a large bell upon each tender, to which shall be attached a cord of a length equal to the maximum length of the train; this vegetable or metallic cord is to be rolled upon a drum placed in the last car, and by means of a mechanism, which is quite complicated, the bell can be sounded. The clearing house should see that every car is furnished with this arrangement, in order that the desired result may be obtained; without this general application the design would be without effect.

It will thus be seen, that the committee did not take into consideration the experience of the French, German, or Belgian engineers; they did not deign to refer to the locomotive mirror, or any other arrangements that have been tried on many roads.

Whence arises this singular difference of opinion? A statistical investigation can alone settle this question. For that, we must have a description in detail of contrivances to effect this object, indicating the time they were brought into use, the services they have rendered in collisions, the security they promise, and the chances of deterioration to which they are subject, and the opinions and observations of all engineers should be compared.

The result of this examination would show that the English are wrong, or that the means at present employed are altogether superfluous.

To enter, at present, into the details of all these contrivances, and to examine designs and models of them would not lead to any definite result. Whatever opinion might be formed on the subject, those of the opposite opinion would deny its justice; thus the clearing house, instead of confining itself to superficial researches, should have communicated the result of its labors to those who furnished the original designs; it would then have had the merit of instituting a general investigation, which alone can decide these controverted questions, and in the mean time, it should give the railroad engineers of all countries the credit of equal capacity.

CHAPTER XXI.

COMPANIES OF INSURANCE AGAINST ACCIDENTS.

As railroad accidents have increased, they have become the subjects of speculation, and companies of Insurance against accidents have been proposed like those against fire and shipwreck. This has been done in

ENGLAND.

England has an institution for the insurance of persons against accidents on railroads. It is the Railway Passenger Assurance Company of London, incorporated in 1849, by an act of Parliament. This company has a capital of four million six hundred thousand dollars; it effects insurance on passengers and persons employed on all railroads in the United Kingdom, giving in consideration of premium paid a fixed sum to the heirs of persons killed upon the railroad, and a proportional sum in cases of injury.

With some rare exceptions, all railroads make an annual contribution to this establishment. To enable the public to partake of its advantages, policies of insurance are sold with the tickets at the stations. These policies are of two kinds; policies for a single trip, called single assurance policies, and temporary policies, or periodical assurances, as their name indicates, for a certain fixed period.

In the fixing of the premium, the length of the route is not taken into consideration; the class of cars only is considered; and the following scale has been fixed.

PASSENGERS INSURED FOR ONE TRIP.

Class of Carriage.	Sum Insured.	Premium.
First Class	$4,600	$5.50 cts.
Second, and Pleasure Trips . .	2,300	3.68 "
Third Class	920	1.84 "

PASSENGERS INSURED FOR A PERIOD OF TIME.

	Premium to be paid for an Insurance of	
Duration of Insurance in Months.	$4,600	$920
1	$1.10	
3	2.20	
6	3.50	
12	4.60	$1.00

From the first of these tables it is seen, that in England, the danger is considered proportional to the inferiority of the car. In insurances for a stated time, no distinction is made in the class of cars.

The above-mentioned sums are paid, in cases of death, to the heirs of the deceased. In cases of injury, the person insured receives a sum proportional to the amount insured and the gravity of his wounds. This indemnity may when necessary be fixed by arbitration.

Besides this the company has an agreement with

many railroads to insure those employed upon them by the year at the following rates.

ANNUAL INSURANCE OF PERSONS EMPLOYED.

Class of Persons.	Sum Insured.	Premiums.
1st. Engine Drivers and Firemen,	$276.00	$10.58
2d. Conductors and Brakemen,	230.00	4.42
3d. Factors, Watchmen, Gatekeepers,	184.00	1.21

Besides these sums stipulated in case of death, each *employé* receives from the insurance company assistance while he is laid up with wounds.

The third and last species of insurance is that of persons travelling much upon railroads; such as travelling mail agents, persons in charge of cattle, who are entitled, in consideration of an annual premium of $4.60, to a weekly allowance of $9.20 until their wounds are healed, and in case of death $920 are paid to their heirs.

Such are the principal arrangements of this society, which is becoming more popular every day.

Although the English laws, like those of France, make the companies and their agents responsible, and inflict heavy damages, when a serious act of negligence has been committed, occasioning death or injury to passengers, accidents frequently happen, which cannot be traced directly to the fault of the company, and the causes of which cannot be determined in a perfectly clear manner; in such cases, the insurance society, not specially interested in the railroad, affords remedies which cannot be obtained by law.

We give some details of the business of this company:—

During the two years, 1850–1851, six insured persons lost their lives; four engine drivers, one superintendent of track, and one conductor; and their families received the sums for which their lives were insured. In the same period, one hundred and twenty-three persons who had been injured, have been paid sums, the enumeration of which will show the tariff of rates. $1,840 for the fracture of a thigh; $920 for a broken arm; $1,104 for loss of an eye; $552.00 for wounds in the head; $110.40 for a broken jaw, and in that proportion.

Those slightly wounded, received from $4.60 to $46.00.

GERMANY.

A plan for mutual insurance was presented in 1850, to the German railroad companies. Its object was to equalize, among all the railroads, the damages resulting from the various accidents that occur in working a road, to the furniture, freight, baggage, fixtures, and rolling stock. Persons were not insured by this association.

The heavy premiums paid by railroads to fire insurance companies, gave rise to this association.

The first company for insurance upon German roads was formed at Erfurt in Prussia, in 1853, under the name of *Thuringia*, with a capital of $1,288,000. It insures persons travelling and serving upon all the railroads of Europe, either for a single trip, a day, or for any fixed time.

This society has the confidence of the public, and has extended its operations over the north of Germany and into a part of Bavaria.

REGULATIONS OF THE THURINGIA INSURANCE COMPANY.

This company insures passengers, *employés*, and mail agents, against all accidents which may happen to them on any of the regular trains, upon any of the railroads of Europe.

These accidents include collisions, burning of cars, damage by lightning, running off the track, breaking down of cars, breaking of axles, wheel tires, springs, and other pieces, falling in of tunnels, falling down of bridges or embankments, explosions of boilers, breaking of cables on inclined planes, bad arrangement of the trains, and falling from the cars either in getting in or getting out. The regular trip, in conformity with the hour of starting, begins at the signal for starting, and ends with the signal of arrival.

The insured person, in case of accident, receives

1st. A temporary assistance.

2d. An indemnity paid at once.

3d. The amount of the sum insured.

Temporary assistance, includes the payment of all expenses in case of sickness, and fifty per cent. of this sum in addition, as compensation for loss of time. If these two amounts exceed the amount for which the life is insured, the injured person shall only receive fifteen per cent. of this sum.

The indemnity paid at once shall be regulated by the following tariff.

1st. The loss of both arms, or both hands, or both feet, or both eyes, seventy-five per cent. of the sum to be paid in case of death.

2d. Loss of the right eye, right arm, or right hand, sixty per cent. of the same sum.

3d. Loss of the left hand, left arm, or a foot, fifty per cent.

4th. Loss of the left eye, thirty per cent.

For any other mutilations, the company will only pay the sum fixed for temporary assistance in cases of illness.

The whole amount is only paid to the heirs, when death occurs within two months after the accident, or when an entire incapacity to labor is produced by it. If an account of the accident, duly certified, is transmitted to the company within three days, the amount insured will be deposited in the *bureau*, to be paid on the presentation of the annual report. Points in dispute are to be settled by arbitration.

The premiums are as follows.

$2\frac{2}{10}$	cents,	for an	insurance	for	$1,362.00	for	1 day.
$4\frac{4}{10}$	"	"	"	"	1,362.00	"	2 days.
$5\frac{1}{2}$	"	"	"	"	3,604.00	"	1 day.
11	"	"	"	"	3,604.00	"	2 days.
$4.05		"	"	"	4,084.00	"	1 year.
6.81		"	"	"	6,808.00	"	" "

Persons can be insured for smaller sums by making special agreements.

Policies are issued by the depot masters of railroads, and by special agents of the company.

This society had hardly been constituted when a

similar society was formed in Berlin upon a more extended basis. This company insures against accidents happening to travellers, to *employés*, to the furniture and working stock, to freight, and the fixed property of the roads. Here are the general arrangements of the company:—

Regulations of the General Association for insurance against *accidents* on railroads.

This society undertakes to insure against accidents resulting from fire, lightning, inundations, and other injuries done by water, slides, explosions of locomotive boilers, collisions, breaking down of cars, running off the track, and, finally, from the breaking of axles and of tires.

It does not insure against those accidents which are the results of war, of the employment of an armed force, of revolts or revolutions, of earthquakes, of gross faults committed by those managing railroads, or against those occasioned by the fault of the passenger.

This society is free to take part in the examination into the causes of any accident. The administration of the road, upon which it may happen, shall give them every assistance. The necessary forms having been complied with, all claims against it, will be paid in one week after the accounts have been arranged. All claims for damages not made within three months of the occurrence of the accident, shall be null and void. The administration of the road, upon which any accident occurs, engages to render all possible assistance, and to notify the insurance company of it at once.

The nature of the wounds shall be determined by the physician attached to the railroad. This society shall have the right, when it sees fit, to have this settled by a consultation of medical men.

The tariff of indemnity is fixed as follows: —

1st. Wounds disabling one from work during eight days, from 75 cents to $6.80.

2d. Wounds disabling one from work for a prolonged period; from $6.80 to $128.00.

3d. Wounds occasioning the loss of one or more limbs, from $128.00 to $736.00.

4th. Wounds disabling one from work during the remainder of life; $736.00 to 1,472.00.

5th. Accidents followed by death, $2,208.00.

Any one can, if he pleases, insure his life at a higher rate.

The particular sum to be paid in any case, shall be fixed between the above-mentioned limits, by the insurance company, and the managers of the railroad upon which the accident happens.

The premium of insurance is paid by the railroad directly, or by the passenger in an increased price for his ticket; it is

$1\frac{1}{10}$ cents for a trip from $4\frac{1}{2}$ miles to $46\frac{1}{2}$ miles.
$2\frac{2}{10}$ cents for a trip above $46\frac{1}{2}$ miles.

Half of this premium belongs to the insurance company; the other half goes to the fund for the relief of *employés*, out of which are paid indemnities in case of injuries, as well as suitable pensions to the families of those who may be killed.

If no accident happens in the course of operating

any road, the society having then nothing to pay, pledges itself to give a sum equal to fifty per cent. of its profits, to the *employés* of the road, as a gratuity.

When an agreement of this nature is made with any road, it shall continue in force one year; and it may then be prolonged.

If any railroad is compelled by the courts to pay damages for accidents greater than those given by this company, this company pledges itself to pay the surplus.

We have now examined three classes of insurance companies, differing from each other in many essential points.

The Mutual Society, not yet carried into operation, which proposes to insure property, and has nothing to do with persons. The *Thuringia*, which only insures passengers and agents upon regular trains, — and the General Society of Berlin, which combines the insurance of passengers, without respect to the kind of train, with that of *employés* and the fixed and movable property of railroads.

FRANCE.

France has, at present, no society of this description; the idea only, belongs to her; a plan for mutual insurance among the directors of all railroads, as well for passengers as for *employés*, having been proposed, some years ago, to our companies, who rejected it, and gave to England the glory of putting it into execution for the benefit of the public. The conception of this plan belongs to M. Blaise (des

Vosges) principal editor of the Journal des Chemins de Fer.

The preceding statements will suffice to give France the basis for similar associations, if the need of such is felt. At present the morality of such institutions is questioned, because they speculate in wounds, mutilations, and death. It is true there is something shocking in placing a money value upon portions of our bodies; but, setting aside this painful sentiment, passengers and *employés* carry with them a certain tranquillity of mind which is always of great value in the trials of life; they know, that by paying a certain premium, they will secure the money and assistance they will need in case of wounds, and accidents, which they can neither foresee nor avoid. On this account, these new institutions are worthy of attention, and as they already exist in England and Germany, we have every reason to think, they will eventually be established in France. The question of their use is not urgent; it will be settled by time, and by the force of circumstances. This volume will fall, perhaps, into the hands of some capitalist, who will see in the establishment of a company for insurance against accidents on railroads, a suitable investment for his funds, and will realize profits from it, as our neighbors across the channel have already done. When this time comes, the information which we have given, may become of some practical utility.

CHAPTER XXII.

STATISTICS OF ACCIDENTS.

VERY few useful and complete statistics have been given to the public. The English occupy, in this department, incontestably the first rank. The railroad commissioners give, in their Annual Report, a very exact account of accidents, entering into all the details, and giving explanatory papers, with plans and profiles of the portion of line, upon which the accident happened. With these documents, engineers can inform themselves of all the circumstances of these accidents, and the measures to be taken to prevent them.

The government of Baden, have also published a statement of facts.

The Belgian government, did the same when its lines were first opened; it is to be regretted that they have discontinued the publication since 1848.

The government of the United States of America have published a book very interesting, and but little known in Europe; it is entitled, A Report of a Committee, appointed by the Senate to examine into the Causes of Accidents upon Railroads, and to point out the Means of preventing them. (Published at Albany.) A complete translation of this document, would doubtless be very useful; but not having met with it, until the plan of my book was arranged, I am obliged to delay this work. I subjoin a brief analysis of it.

The report, presented in the name of the committee by the state engineer, and the chairman of the railroad committee on the part of the senate, divides the causes of accidents into three classes: defects in the way and the rolling stock; irregularity in the working of the road; and obstructions on the track.

As defects of construction, they point out in the first place, — premature opening of roads, where they are not ballasted through their whole extent. Gravel trains are then moving over the line, together with passenger and freight trains, and are not always placed upon the side tracks at the proper time; pieces of masonry and bridges are left unfinished, and have not the strength requisite for use; grade crossings are not properly watched or guarded, and the rails are of bad quality or too light. In general the road is not so substantial as it should be, taking into consideration the weight and speed of the trains; and the danger is increased on heavy grades and sharp curves, especially when the rails are affected by frost. At such a time the locomotive seems to *root up* the track.

The committee is of opinion, that with the loads and speeds now used, the public is not secure, and demands that railroads should be constructed in a more substantial manner.

The cars seem to be sufficient for the protection of the passengers; but, in cases of axles breaking, the flooring is not strong enough to prevent the broken axle from coming through and wounding the passengers. Besides this, axles and wheels ought never to be used on passenger cars more than one year. They may be used, after this, upon freight cars.

On examination of this American book, it will be seen that there are marked differences between the rolling stock of the United States and that of Europe. Cast-iron wheels are often used there, but they are frequently broken by frost. The brakes are sometimes badly attached, and falling on the track, throw off the train. The committee therefore regrets the want of powerful brakes.

As a means of preventing accidents, the committee can only propose great strictness in enforcing rules. Incompetent persons are too often employed to satisfy the demands of the stockholders or the public, and this is, according to the report, the most common cause of accidents. As a legislative measure, it was advised that railroads should be placed under the immediate surveillance of the State, by giving to the agents of the government, the right to make more strict investigations into all the details of the construction and working of railroads.

The second part of this American work, contains under the name of an Appendix, a series of questions addressed to companies, on the affairs of their roads, and on all accidents, as well as answers from many of the roads. Tables of statistics complete the report.

In order that these statistics of accidents should be made useful and lead to practical results, they should be undertaken in all countries; for an universal statistic, can alone indicate the course to pursue in order to arrive at a solution of problems, which theoretical science, in its present state, cannot give. A simple enumeration of the number of persons killed and wounded, of passengers and *employés*, is not enough; that can only furnish a number of figures, susceptible of an infinite number of combinations as regards the amount of travel, the class of cars, the length of time the roads have been open, etc.; for these figures, though of interest to the curious, give no real, practical information.

They may, however, give confidence to passengers, by showing that accidents are very rare upon railroads when compared with other modes of conveyance; this result appears from an investigation of all the accidents which have happened upon English roads from 1840 to 1852, and which have been published in the official reports of the London Statistical Society. In this period of twelve years, 1,828 persons have been killed, and 2,648 have been wounded: —

	Killed.	Wounded.
Passengers	266	1.796
Persons not connected with the road .	175	65
Persons standing on the track . .	306	84
Engine drivers	73	94
Firemen	116	123
Conductors	126	100
Watchmen and brakemen . . .	117	65
Other *employés*	648	321
Total	1,828	2,648

According to this table, the number of passengers

killed (266) is as 1 to 2,300,000 persons carried; and the number wounded (1796) as 1 to 340,000. The proportion of killed to wounded is as 1 to 7. Four fifths of those injured, while standing on the track, were killed.

The English Statistical Society classifies accidents, also, according to their causes. At the beginning of this period, from 1840 to 1852, eight per cent. of the accidents causing death were occasioned by the breaking of axles. The 308 collisions were caused, 28 by bad weather, 34 by defects in the material of the track, engines, or cars, 8 by deficiency of motive power, 238 by inattention or negligence on the part of *employés*.

These collisions were: 48 between passenger trains; 207 between passenger and freight trains; 53 between freight trains.

Referring to the rates of speed, it is remarked, that fewer accidents happen to express trains than others; the reason of this is, that these trains have better engines and are managed by the most skilful engine drivers, and the attention of those in charge of the track is specially directed to its condition, whenever an express train is expected. Of these 308 collisions, 110 occurred at stations.

The cause of trains running off the track is most frequently a bad state of the rails, which are kept in repair by contract.

Setting aside their terrible consequences, it is mainly the causes of all these accidents, which it is important to study.

We must attempt to discover why it is, that on

certain lines accidents are more frequent than upon others in the same condition as regards construction and traffic, and we should inform ourselves of the different modes of working roads in different countries. It is known, for example, that in Germany the trains are often delayed, and many *employés* are wounded; that France is the theatre of great catastrophes, happening at long intervals, but that in other respects the management is satisfactory; that in England, accidents are very frequent, so as to excite the attention of parliament, investigations have been had, but while the fact has been settled, attention has only been paid to palliatives. Sometimes it is thought that a greater latitude should be given to the control and coercive measure adopted by the companies, who demand that the whole responsibility should be laid upon the superintendent; sometimes there is a fear of restraining the liberty of trade and industry by the application of these measures. The courts subject the companies and their *employés* to severe penalties, and yet the accidents do not diminish in number or gravity; on the contrary they increase as the rolling stock and the track suffers wear and deterioration, which the companies, loaded with debt, cannot make good. They see their profits daily diminishing in consequence of ruinous competition, which the amalgamation of different lines is powerless to stop. By reducing the number and speed of their trains, they of course expose themselves to fewer chances of accident; but the English public does not go into details, and demands, on the contrary, more trains and a higher rate of speed.

According to the report of the Board of Trade, 45 millions of passengers have passed over the railroads of Great Britain during the first half of the year 1853. 148 persons have been killed, and 191 wounded in all. Of these 31 were killed and 141 wounded in consequence of forty serious accidents, which are divided into 18 collisions, 11 runnings off the track, 5 breakings of locomotive axles, 2 breakings of car axles, and 4 explosions of locomotive boilers.

Without multiplying these statements, it will be seen, that a general statistical account would probably lead to the discovery of the causes of these accidents; whether they depend on local customs, the exigencies of passengers, which must of course be satisfied; on mechanical arrangements, or on the character and habits of the men who manage the trains. We shall see perhaps, that the number of these accidents depend upon the character of the *employés*, and that with a body of men contented with their situations, there is much less risk, than with agents discontented with their lot, and tired of their duties; for what confidence can be placed in men badly directed, who place no value upon the opinions of their chief, and who despise the experience of their comrades?

It seems to me that the seat of the evil is to be found here, and I do not hesitate to repeat it even to weariness. On a railroad, the *employé* is often a willing instrument, but his superior must know how to manage him, and it is in this that the talents of railroad superintendents lie. In being able to find capable men, in knowing how to make themselves beloved by their subordinates, and in obtaining regularity in the service, not so much by fear as by devotion.

If the Paris and Strasbourg Railroad Company had not applied this rule with that intelligence, of which its committee give daily proofs, we should not have found an engine driver, who in the late severe weather, kept in his hands a detached piece of the engine, and brought his train into the station at the proper time with his hands frozen. Such acts of devotion are not found upon all lines.

The reports of a railroad, near our frontier, state that during ten years, only one serious accident has occurred; it was owing to the carelessness of the engine driver, who, not slackening his speed on coming on to a side track, run into a train standing there. A legal investigation showed that this engine driver was a careless man, who had committed many faults upon other roads and been discharged for them.

Should a train be intrusted to such a man? If a careless man must never be kept upon a railroad, there should not be too much severity and especially no arrogance or pride on the part of their superiors. On a German road I have seen a simple depot master insult an engine driver as Russian officers insult their soldiers. Nothing irritates the *employés* of a public service so much as being treated with disdain; nothing wounds them more, for arrogant airs are often the mask of incapacity.

As relates to men employed on the road, there are no precise rules; every company, every engineer acts in his own way; and as the condition of the *employés* is not the same, their manner of performing their duties is not the same, and yet it ought to be such as will secure regularity in running the trains.

Orders are often conceived in too vague a manner, giving too great latitude of interpretation to subordinate agents. Uniformity in this most important point should be secured.

Such are the important questions in regard to the construction and management of railroads, and the character of *employés*, that the statistics of accidents will enable us to decide. It is a great task that I have undertaken, but I will venture to say, that the day will come, when railroad accidents will become impossible, and then these new modes of communication and transport will have reached the end which the genius of civilization designed for them.

I am now approaching the end of my work, which is to give a concise statement of the means necessary to introduce regularity into the working of roads, by which alone accidents can be avoided.

CHAPTER XXIII.

SUMMARY.

I do not pretend to point out an universal and infallible method of preserving railroads from accidents. I do not believe it to be possible, at least at present; for this great machine of transport is composed of two elements, whose simultaneous action cannot be combined in an absolute manner:—the regular working of mechanism, and the carefulness and intelligence of men. Besides, for negligence and imprudence on the part of passengers, there is no remedy, unless we perform the duties of men by mechanical contrivances, and treat them like freight, by closing them up, as was once done, in boxes, and not allowing them any movements which might possibly be injurious to them; and even then we should not arrive at a satisfactory result.

For the breaking down and collisions of trains, no absolute preventive measures can be taken. We should avoid complications in the service, and too difficult combinations of trains; those concerned in working the road, should be subjected, above all things, to a strict and intelligent control.

To prevent, as much as possible, trains from running off the track, all the details of the way should be subjected to an active and continual surveillance. In the observation of signals, which are generally given with great exactness, every thing depends upon the engine driver.

The rules of the road should be made as perfect as possible; the services which may be rendered by the electric telegraph, and the practical value of those so-called certainties which are based on suppositions, and which so often give rise to accidents, should be considered. We should examine especially what has been done in other countries, and not rest satisfied with our own experience, however great that may be; or base our operations upon preconceived ideas or theoretical plans.

In fine, we should fix our attention upon two points; the improvement of the stock of our roads, and a careful selection of *employés*.

To reach the first result, the efforts of all engineers and constructors should be centralized, still keeping in view isolated experiments; and so much the more, as they are generally made in a disinterested spirit and for a useful end. As to the working of roads, properly so called, the French government has addressed a series of questions, which all the companies will answer. It is to be desired that this should be imitated by others, who could thus coöperate in a work, which is meritorious in more than one point of view.

Already many matters, which were the subjects of serious reflections and reasonable fears, have been settled; means have been found for fixing the rails firmly, and giving a great stability to the rolling stock.

Other problems should be investigated; and, to

enhance the value of this work, I repeat, that all engineers should consider them, and work out their ideas to some common end. This may be done, without any serious difficulty, by preparing a sort of programme of the doubtful points. This programme, the form of which is indifferent, might be very easily composed; it would include a series of questions on the construction of the roads, and of the superstructure, on the manufacture and strength of the engines and cars, and answers to them should be sent to societies of engineers, and finally examined by an international committee. From this would arise a sort of railway congress.

The carrying out of this plan would really cost nothing, and to it might be added the collection of complete statistics of railroads, and especially of the causes of accidents; it would stimulate the zeal of all persons concerned in the construction and working of roads, and would cause the science in which we are all interested to advance one step at least.

To effect this object, any society of engineers has only to put itself into communication with other societies; one member might communicate with the societies of France or of England, another with those of Prussia, another with those of Austria; and as no society would refuse to answer to the call, the opinions of all could be made common, and practical conclusions might be drawn from them, which might afterwards be given to the public. All this seems very easy to me, and it is astonishing that it has not been done before this time.

While waiting for the realization of this idea, I will commence by opening the first page of a register, in which I will inscribe the following questions, whose solution would, without doubt, add to the security of railroad travel.

1st. The explosion of locomotive boilers is not a common occurrence; with some precautions it can be prevented; What means, and what contrivances, can be used to insure safety?

2d. The breaking of axles is very rare, especially in France, where the modes of manufacture have attained a high degree of perfection. In Germany it is more common.

Is this difference caused by a difference in the iron, in the manufacture, or in the use?

To decide when an axle is beginning to break, we need only heat it, from time to time, in a slow fire, after having rubbed it with oil, which will enter the fissure, and come out when it cools. The zeal of the *employés* might be stimulated by giving a reward to all who pointed out an axle not fit for use.

Is there any other more effectual way of detecting these commencing ruptures, or of avoiding evil consequences when they break?

3d. The stability of locomotives may be secured by counterweights. What is the best mode of applying them?

4th. With fixed attachments to the rails, and with the compound rail, solutions of continuity in the track are avoided. Why is this mode of attachment not used in France? Why is it used with reserve in England? Why does Germany reject chairs, and place on all its roads the American rail with screw-plates? In general, why are the opinions of intelligent engineers so divided on this subject?

What practical conclusion can be drawn from the solution of these questions?

5th. Bridges of cast and of wrought iron form the subject of controversy. What are the facts in support of the opposite opinions? Are there any reasons for using one of these systems in preference to the other?

6th. Can the causes of rails breaking be determined? What measures can be taken to prevent it?

7th. Which are preferable, switches moved by hand, or by counterweights?

8th. The questions relating to collisions, signals, and single track roads, are intimately connected. The electric telegraph plays a very important part here. On this subject, a question of principle has has been lately raised in a paper of the Society of Civil Engineers of Paris: it is there said that the electric telegraph does not render eminent services to railroads unless it is placed exclusively under their charge, and explains the rapid progress that has been made in this department in Germany, by the fact that the government have nothing to do with the management of this mode of communication.

I have consulted, on this subject, "The General Statistics of the German Railroads," published by a convention of their managers. I find there proof to the contrary.

The length of the German railroads is 6,214 miles, of which 2,796 belong to the following governments:

Austria, 932 miles; Prussia, 590 miles; Bavaria, 373 miles; Saxony, 248.5; Hanover, 248.5; Wurtemburg, 155 miles; Baden, 174 miles; Brunswick, 75 miles.

All these government lines are furnished with the electric telegraph, whilst those belonging to incorporated companies do not have them through their whole extent. The common travelled roads do not have them.

Thus the assertion quoted above is not in conformity with the official documents. It was not for the purpose of refuting an opinion published by a member of the Society of Civil Engineers, that I have entered upon this investigation, but to add another to my list of questions.

What is the part the electric telegraph should play in the working of railroads with single or double tracks?

9th. The electric telegraph leads me to speak of the electric chimes placed on the guard-houses, to signalize the approach of trains which have not been announced; and the electric fire, to take the place of explosive signals, the inefficiency of which has been felt.

In generalizing this question: What advantage can be derived from inventions made, not so much for the purpose of preventing accidents, as for diminishing their injurious results?

The number of these questions can be increased by those propounded in a book just published by Mr. Couche on Collisions.

It seems to me of use to transcribe these questions, fourteen in number, in addition to those that I have given above.

10th. At the moment when a train quits a station, should it be signalized to the train that is to follow on a double track, as is necessarily practised on a single track?

11th. Should the passage of a train be announced to all engaged on the track, or only to those who are placed in charge of dangerous points; such as curves, branches, grade crossings?

12th. Should the use of disc signals be made general at grade crossings? Is all the advantage taken of signals that should be, at switches placed at the entrance of stations?

13th. Should the use of fixed signals cease at night, when the signal is neither visible at the station-house, nor placed at a point where the guard can constantly watch over the condition of the lantern?

14th. Is it useful to have in stations an indicator at each switch?

15th. Should the running of extra trains be restrained to cases of absolute necessity, when they cannot be announced at the stations and dangerous points on the track?

16th. Should assisting service be organized on the demand of a train in distress? and should such a train have the liberty of asking for assistance in either direction?

17th. To what extent is it possible to compel every train to leave for itself, at certain fixed distances, and particularly at the commencement of curves, a mark of its having passed, to warn the train following, until it shall become useless by the arrival of the watchman?

Cannot this be done without the intervention of any mechanical contrivance?

18th. Cannot this arrangement be easily made, at least by freight trains, that is, by those trains of whose passage such an indication would be particularly useful?

19th. Cannot the electric light be made use of for the night signals, and especially in cases of fog, and thus restore to signals directed to the eye a part of their efficacy?

20th. Are the watchmen always in sufficient numbers? Are they always proportional to the condition of the track, and especially to the number of trains during the day and at night?

21st. The daily work of engine drivers, and the length of single trips they have to make, do they ever exceed the proper limits, especially during unpleasant weather? Does not cold wind and rain, after some hours, paralyze to a certain point the attention which should always be on the alert, where a single instant of forgetfulness may cost so dear?

22d. Are the number of side tracks sufficient for the freight trains? Is the establishment of intermediate side tracks, away from the stations, advisable upon lines of great traffic?

23d. Are the brakes, supposing them to be in good condition, sufficiently numerous? Is not a brake indispensable on the last car, on sections of the road where the inclines are of great length?

This *programme* contains twenty-three questions, many of which have received approximate solutions.

I will not push my researches any further. I have restricted myself to presenting a plan, which cannot be completed except by the concurrent labor of all engineers.

There is, besides those mentioned, a number of accidents arising from carelessness, which may escape the investigation of the most conscientious, which cannot be covered by the orders of the superintendent, or guarded against by the attention of the agents under him. How, in fact, can accidents be foreseen, occasioned by things falling on the rails; by cattle breaking through the fences; by carriages stopping on grade crossings; by loaded wagons, whose height has not been measured, through forgetfulness, by passing them under the gauge; by the chimneys of locomotives striking against scaffoldings at the entrance of depots, or other works under repair, which breaking, fall upon the *employés*, and stop the progress of the train; by cars at stations driven out of place by the wind, or left by chance upon the track? In these matters, we must depend entirely upon the intelligence of the passengers, and the circumspection of the *employés*.

CHAPTER XXIV.

CONCLUSION.

NOTWITHSTANDING the impossibility of pointing out definite measures to avoid accidents, there are modes of improving the working of roads, which we will, for practical purposes, point out in the five following propositions: —

1st. The most serious attention should be paid to the selection of those to be employed on the road, and the duties of every agent should be distinctly defined (see the accident at Poitiers); and the superintendent should have the authority to discharge any persons whose duties and position are not precisely defined, so that confusion may be avoided.

2d. Devotion to the interests of the road should be stimulated among all subordinate agents, by making their positions comfortable. Careless, discontented persons, and those showing any desire to leave, should be discharged at once; this, unfortunately, is not practised with sufficient energy. A railroad is a machine of transport, and should never be made a paternal and benevolent institution for persons who do not perform the duties required of them.

3d. Frequent inspections should be made, like those on the Northern road. A commission of the superior officers of this company visits, from time to time, the stations and other posts of the road, and examines all the *employés* in the details of their duties, in the working of signals and of the telegraph.

No sooner is the rumor of this inspection spread abroad, than all employed on the road hasten to study the regulations, and exercise themselves in all the departments of their duties. Everybody gains by this: capable servants are distinguished; and direct intercourse with the superintendent does away with the necessity of many letters and circulars.

4th. To establish conferences of all the engineers of the country, and to promote international conventions, to carry out the plan I have proposed.

5th. To create a board of universal statistics, to combine the labors of all engineers, so that they may be subjected to criticism and given to the public.

I would now say a few words to the public. Formerly passengers took their seats in the cars with patience and resignation. Now the feeling which animates them is impatience, and if this is not satisfied with a rate of speed, of which some years since we had not even the idea, it is changed to ill will against the agents of this new mode of conveyance.

In many cases, the public suspects the whole administration, from the directors to the watchmen, of negligence and incapacity. It considers nothing, excuses nothing, and often comprehends nothing. It forgets that railroads exist only through the zeal and devotion of honorable and intelligent men, of whom they take no account. He who has never ridden on a locomotive does not know how much courage, intrepidity, and address is needed to conduct a train.

He only sees a delay, an accident, but he does not see the precautions that are taken at every moment by those in the employ of the company, who have the greatest interest in performing their duties with a zeal and devotion equal to every emergency; for they know the rewards that await them, the punishment which threatens, and the penalties of the law which hang over them.

Unfortunately the press echoes thoughtless prejudices. Let the boilers of steamboats explode; let stages overturn or remain fixed in snow on impracticable roads; let carts, recklessly driven, run over persons in the street, — these things are natural; no attention is paid to them, they are customary.

But let a train run off the track at Zarskœzelo, the journals of Madrid hasten to put the fact on record; let a locomotive run off an embankment at Aranjuez, and the New York papers publish the details, and the Parisian press, as well as that of other capitals, collect together all these stories, and awaken disquietude in the hearts of passengers, and disgust with their duties in the souls of *employés*, which are so cruelly tried in these latter times.

These recitals are neither instructive or amusing. They give no precise information, and it would be better if they were entirely suppressed.

The public should regain its confidence, and dismiss as soon as possible these unfounded prejudices. Railroads, even with the defects inherent in all human works, offer the most certain and rapid mode of conveyance; and no means are left untried to perfect them. In all countries, they are subjects of study with serious minds, and they are every day advancing more nearly to perfection. Besides, where can be found more practical science than among railroad engineers; more intelligence than among railroad managers; or a better staff than those employed in the working of roads? And above all this is placed the solicitude of the government, which watches without cessation over the interests and safety of the people.

APPENDIX

BY THE TRANSLATOR.

APPENDIX.

A.

EXPLOSIONS OF LOCOMOTIVE BOILERS.

BY THE TRANSLATOR.

The construction of the locomotive boiler, renders it less liable to bursting, at other points than the tubes, from the gradual increase in the pressure of steam, than other forms of boiler, and it rarely, if ever, bursts from this cause while it is in motion. When the regulator is open, and a free communication made between the boiler and the cylinders, the steam, as fast as it is generated, passes into the cylinder, and acting upon the piston, which may be considered as a valve, loaded with a weight equal to the resistance of the train, moves it as soon as its pressure equals this resistance with a speed proportionate to the rapidity with which the steam is generated. No load that would be likely to be put upon a locomotive engine would cause a resistance upon the piston greater than the iron of the boiler was able to bear, and until this was done, the piston would move before the boiler burst, giving vent to the steam, and the speed of the train would be increased, until an equilibrium was established between the power of the steam generated, and the resistance of the load. But yet it is found that the boilers of locomotive engines do explode, not only while in motion, but also immediately after the pressure of the steam in the boiler has been, to all appearance, reduced by the opening of the regulator, the raising of the safety-valve, the sounding of the steam whistle, or the introduction of cold water.

Facts seem to warrant the opinion that a very small portion of the explosions of locomotive boilers are occasioned by the gradual increase of the pressure of the steam under an overloaded valve. They seem to be produced by causes which act suddenly and against which no safety-valve, at least as at present arranged, is any safeguard whatever. The circumstances, under which these explosions take place, are various as we propose to show.

An explosion sometimes occurs immediately on the starting of an engine. This may, we think, be produced by two causes, acting either separately or conjointly.

1st. Water, under the pressure of a single atmosphere boils at 212° Fahrenheit, and at other temperatures varying with the pressure. As water, kept perfectly still, may be cooled below the usual freezing point without being frozen, so it may be heated above the usual boiling point, under the same circumstances, without being turned into steam. While a locomotive is standing with the fire burning slowly under the boiler, the pressure of the steam is constantly but slowly increasing, and the water being kept perfectly still may he heated above the boiling point for the given pressure, as it certainly is up to it. As soon however as the regulator is opened, or the safety-valve raised, a portion of the pressure is removed, and rapid ebullition is produced in water heated above the boiling point for this reduced pressure, and a sudden disengagement of steam is produced in the same way as crystals of ice are formed in water cooled below the freezing point, by agitating it. The steam thus rapidly generated, strikes the boiler with a sudden blow, and breaks it, though the boiler would resist perfectly the same force gradually applied.

That this sudden and destructive generation of steam arises at times from a reduction of the pressure, would seem probable from the appearance of boilers after explosion. They are torn in all directions, and rarely, if ever, present the appearance of a single opening relieving at once the internal pressure, like the prick of a pin in a bladder distended with air. Any thing that excites motion in the water may cause this sudden development of steam, as the following facts show.

A stationary engine exploded at Bradford, in England, in 1844. The fire had got down very low, and more fuel was put on. The steam was escaping from the safety-valves. The boiler exploded seven or eight minutes after the fuel was put in. The cause assigned was that the water had been heated when perfectly still above the boiling point by a slow fire, the sudden increase of which putting the water in motion, caused a sudden development of steam.*

An experiment described in the same magazine illustrates the same principle: —

"Take a common Florence flask, about half full of water; boil the water over a lamp; remove the lamp, and when all ebullition has ceased, holding the flask steady, cork it. Take it now by the neck in the hand protected by a cloth, and give it one or two vigorous shakes. The flask will instantly burst with a pretty observable explosion."

2d. While the locomotive is standing, the fire being slow and the water still, the level of the water may be lowered below the smoke tubes, and they may become heated. As soon as the regulator is opened, ebullition becomes quite rapid, and the level of the water may be raised by it two or three

* Mechanic's Magazine, May, 1844.

inches, so as to bring it upon the heated tubes or plates. This will be followed by an instantaneous development of steam, which may burst the boiler.

These sudden and violent explosions more frequently take place while the engine is in motion, as has happened in many cases on American roads. Owing to the carelessness of the engine driver, or faulty construction or working of the pumps, and these are apt to get out of order at high rates of speed, the water having been allowed to get too low in the boiler, the exposed portion of it becomes intensely heated, and water being again admitted, an instantaneous generation of steam follows which tears the boiler in pieces.

Besides the danger of a sudden generation of steam on the introduction of cold water, as the strength of iron is greatly diminished by being heated redhot, (according to Fairbarn it is diminished five sixths), when a portion of the boiler is thus heated it may burst under the ordinary working pressure.

While the engine is running, as in the case of the Taychonic on the Boston and Providence road, on a down grade, with the regulator closed, an explosion of this kind may occur without the introduction of any more water into the boiler, by the opening of the regulator, the raising of the safety-valve or the blowing of the whistle, either of which by increasing the rapidity of ebullition, may raise the level of the water, so as to bring it upon the heated surface. In the case of the Taychonic, the whistle was heard the instant before the explosion, and it seems probable that the accident was caused rather by a change in the level of the water in the boiler, than by an increase of its quantity.

Alfred Guthrie, in a memorial to Congress on the subject of steam boiler explosions, has given an example of one occurring in a stationary boiler from the introduction of water into it, when it was heated, which shows so clearly the mode in which this class of explosions occurs that I shall quote it in full.

"It was an ordinary sized Mississippi boiler used in a machine shop; the water fed to the forcing pump through a side faucet, to be shut off or on at pleasure, leading to a cistern overhead. The regular engineer came to the shop in the morning and started the works; the boiler had been filled and this faucet closed, so that no water found its way to the pumps. Soon after the engineer was taken suddenly ill, leaving the boiler in charge of a person thought to be competent, but who in fact was entirely ignorant of the business. The fire was continued for a short time, every thing going on well, until the water became low and afforded nothing for the generation of steam, when the power began to diminish and the machinery to be driven with enfeebled force. This state of things tended to increase the energy of the firemen, the arch being crowded with fuel without effect, until finally the whole work was upon the point of stopping. At this moment the owner came in, and found an excellent fire and no apparent reason why the engine should not do its accustomed duty. He found by the water gauge that there was no water, and hastened to the side faucet, and imprudently turned on the water, and in an instant the whole was blown to atoms, killing the engineer, and severely injuring many others who were in the building, which it levelled to the ground."

Locomotive boilers may explode from the effects of incrustations forming upon their bottoms or sides. In the engineer's and architect's Journal for September 1854, there is an account of the effects of incrustations upon salt pans, which illustrates the principle very well.

"A crust of salt frequently forms upon the pans. The cessation of ebullition (if the deposit occurred over the furnace) was the consequence, and the bottom of the pan became redhot. The manner in which the scale was disengaged, was to strike it with the edge of a heavy iron pricker, which allowed the brine to reach the plate. It was also frequently broken by the expansion and bagging down of the plates, leaving the crusts above like an arch. In such cases, the plate was seen, for a moment, to be redhot, and immediately afterwards, an immense column of brine was projected from the pan, the steam evidently being of great elasticity.

Mr. Parkes had seen a yard square of the scale burst, the whole surface of the scale being of a glowing heat. Had the pan been closed, like a steam boiler, he conceived that the blow of the steam on the roof, bottom, and sides, would have destroyed the vessel.

A thin plate of copper at Mr Parke's work had a hole burst through it by the sudden action of steam thus generated. He conceived that similar phenomena might and frequently did occur in steam boilers."

These incrustations are constantly forming upon steam boilers, and when they reach a certain thickness, interfere greatly with the transmission of heat; the iron beneath them becomes redhot, and expanding cracks the deposit over it, water is admitted, and explosion occurs in the manner related above.

A careful chemical analysis of these deposits and of the water used, would, we think, indicate means for preventing them, and would thus increase the efficiency and safety of the steam-engine, for the same deposit which causes the danger, diminishes the evaporating power.

If the water spaces at the sides of the fire box are too narrow, steam may be so rapidly generated there, as to drive the water up, and this process would be aided by the property of heated iron to repel water, which from the experiments of the Franklin Institute, seems to commence to show itself at the temperature of 334° Fahrenheit, and to increase rapidly as the temperature rises above that point. This may go on until this part of the boiler, being filled only with dry steam becomes intensely heated. So long as the steam is rapidly generated it will continue to drive the water out of the narrow space, and no evil result will follow, unless the pressure of the steam becomes too great for the resistance of the iron, diminished as it is by the heat. But when, by opening the furnace door, or closing the regulator, the energy of the fire is diminished, and steam is generated less rapidly, the water falling back upon the heated plate, flashes into steam and bursts the boiler.

May 2d, 1848, a stationary engine exploded in Philadelphia from this cause; the explosion taking place after the furnace door was opened and the fire had gone down. A stationary boiler exploded at Middletown, Connecticut, January 26th, 1841, twenty minutes after it had been set in motion. The cause assigned was an undue heating of the space between the fire box and the outer shell, this space being but two and a half inches. The explosion was exceedingly violent, throwing the whole boiler two hundred to two hundred and twenty feet into the air.*

From the peculiar form of locomotive boilers the part referred to being, in them, the narrowest, and at the same time the weakest portion, explosions might arise in them from this cause. Owing also to the position of the different sides of the shell of the boiler at this point, where the inner end of the stay bolt is exposed to the intense heat of the fire, and the outer end to the external air, the irregular expansion and contraction of the iron of which they are composed must tend greatly to change their texture and diminish their strength.

It is difficult, however, in many cases to decide upon the

* Franklin Journal, January, 1842.

precise cause of locomotive explosions. The engineer, who might give the most valuable information, is most frequently killed by the accident, and the causes of the catastrophe can be inferred only from the appearance of the wreck; but it seems perfectly clear that a great majority of them do not arise from a gradual increase of pressure in the boiler, and that against most of them the safety-valve is no protection. In all the cases to which we have alluded, there is one common characteristic. This consists in a sudden, an instantaneous development of a large quantity of steam which the safety-valve, even were the steam to strike it before the injury was done, would be wholly inadequate to give immediate vent to. But in almost all, if not all of these cases, the boiler is burst before the wave occasioned by the sudden generation of steam has had time to strike the valve.

According to Laplace, the conducting power of steam at a pressure of four atmospheres, and a temperature of $294\frac{1}{10}$ Fahrenheit, is 1041.34 feet per second, and of water 6036.88 feet per second. The ratio of these different velocities is 1 to 5.7. If then, owing to a low state of water, the upper tubes were heated, and water suddenly poured upon them from the pumps, the wave occasioned by the sudden generation of steam at the surface of the water would be transmitted down through the water with a velocity $5\frac{3}{4}$ times as great as it would upwards through the steam, and thus burst out the bottom of the boiler, before the safety-valve was touched. When this rapid generation of steam is occasioned by the separation of incrustations, or from narrow side spaces, the bottom or sides of the boiler being so much nearer the origin of the wave, the injury would of course be done before the valve could be reached.

In almost all cases of explosions of locomotive boilers, while in motion, it will be found that the force of the explosion is downwards and is very violent; that it occurs under circumstances that cannot be explained on the theory of a gradually increasing pressure occasioned by an overloaded valve, but that it is caused by a sudden development of power, some of the causes or supposed causes of which we have indicated.

It has been proposed to place a valve at the bottom of the boiler as a safeguard against this peculiar form of explosion, but this suggestion has never, to our knowledge, been carried out. Fusible plugs have been used as a protection against those explosions which are caused by a low state of the water. In France these plugs are formed of alloys of tin and lead with a small quantity of bismuth, in such proportions as will insure fusion at a temperature somewhat below that of molten lead. Great importance is attached to these alloys, and in order to secure certainty as to their proportions, they are prepared at the mint. Fairbarn advises the use of a lead rivet, one inch in diameter, immediately over the fireplace, and is of opinion that the less frequent occurrence of boiler explosions in France, than in England, is owing to the fact that in the former country the fusible plug is more frequently used.

The only other means of safety at present available are care on the part of the engine driver, that the water is kept at its proper level, and the boiler is free from incrustations, and on the part of the engine builder that the side spaces and the spaces between the tnbes are made so wide, as to prevent the steam forcing all the water out of them and thus bringing about the same state of things at the bottom of the boiler as a low state of water does at the top.

B.

Locomotive engines are usually worked at a pressure of from 80 to 100 pounds to the inch, and taking one of the usual construction, we shall find at 100 pounds to the inch, that it rushes forward on the rail with a pent-up force within its interior of nearly 60,000 tons, which is rather increased than diminished at an accelerated speed.*

C.

CARELESSNESS OF EMPLOYÉS.

The following extract from the Massachusetts Railroad Reports shows how much confusion and what serious accidents the carelessness of one man may give rise to.

On the 3d of March, 1847, during a period when the whole operations of the road were confined to a single track, in consequence of the taking up of the other track, for the purpose of laying down a new and heavier rail, a collision took place between a descending passenger train and an empty gravel train, which was ascending on the same track. This collision was occasioned by the careless inattention of the engineman, who had the train in charge, in immediately leaving Worcester on the arrival of an upward freight train, without taking notice of the customary signal borne by that

* Lectures on the steam-boiler by William Fairbarn, C. E.

train, indicating that another train was following in its rear. The consequences of the collision were, a considerable injury to the engine and cars, and a serious personal injury to a passenger, who had, without authority, taken a stand upon the platform of the baggage car. All the persons on the gravel train saved themselves from injury, by jumping from it before the collision; the engineman having first taken the precaution to reverse his engine, but not to shut off the steam. From the effect of the shock and the power of the steam, the engine was immediately set in motion in an opposite direction, before the engineman could regain his station upon it. It ran down the road a distance of eight miles, when it stopped from the exhaustion of the steam. It was there soon unexpectedly encountered by the four o'clock passenger train from Boston, when another collision took place, with some damage to the *materiel* of the two trains, but without any personal injury. On the coming up subsequently of the steamboat train, the disabled parts of the injured train were removed from the track, and the two passenger trains being united in one, they proceeded onwards towards Worcester. The track being still obstructed by the wrecks of the first collision, it became necessary to pass over the newly laid track which was nearly finished but not reopened for use. While proceeding slowly and with great caution upon this track, on approaching the freight station, the train, from the darkness of the night, came in contact with some freight cars which had been placed on the track while it was disused, and which the agent had not succeeded in removing; and by this collision two other persons, a road-repairer and a baggage-master, were seriously injured. The former died of his wounds, but the latter recovered. This series of disasters arose from the culpable momentary heedlessness of an agent, of good character and capacity, who had been for some time employed in the same situation and who had inspired confidence by his prudence and good conduct. He was, of course, discharged from his situation.*

D.

CRYSTALLIZATION OF WROUGHT IRON.

The peculiar change in wrought iron, indicated in chapter XI., has been also noticed in England, and it is a subject well worthy the most careful examination, at this time when wrought iron is every day becoming more and more used. That certain causes produce a change in the iron by which its strength is greatly diminished, and its fibrous quality destroyed, without any perceptible external change, the observations both in England and France leave us no room to doubt; and it is of the last importance, that these causes should be well defined, and if possible, the time during which wrought iron can be subjected to them without incurring risk of fracture, determined by observation and experiment. The fracture of axles of locomotives and cars is not uncommon, and many lives have been destroyed by this accident, which has frequently happened in the ordinary working of the road, without any increase in the average load or speed, and without any previous sign of weakness. The experiments related in chapter XI., show that when subjected to shocks and torsions wrought iron has a tendency to assume a crystalline state, and become brittle: this change may also

* Sixteenth Annual Report of the Boston and Worcester Railroad Corporation.

be produced by magnetism and heat, and by the process of manufacture.

Mr. Hood, at a meeting of the Institution of Civil Engineers in England, stated that a large anchor, which had been in store for more than a century at Woolwich Dock, and was supposed to be made of extremely good iron, had been recently tested as an experiment, and had broken instantly with a comparatively small strain. The fracture presented large crystals. In this case, Mr. Hood believed that this effect was produced by magnetic influences dependent on the length of time the iron had been in the same position.

Mr. Low, stated that at the gas works under his direction, wrought iron fire bars, though more expensive, were generally preferred. A pan of water was kept beneath them, the steam from which would speedily cause them to become magnetic. He had frequently seen these bars, when thrown down, break into three pieces, with a large crystalline fracture. The same change may be produced in any piece of wrought iron by heating and rapidly cooling it by dipping it in water for a few times.

This change is also often produced in iron by hammering it when below a welding heat, and in forging intricate pieces of iron-work, the ends have frequently been jarred off while the other parts were being hammered. The larger the piece of iron is, the more difficult it is to keep it at an uniform heat, and the more likely this change is to take place; and we have lately learned from an English paper, that "Mr. Nasmyth's wrought iron gun has proved a complete failure; and this, not on account of the mechanical difficulties which had to be encountered — formidable as they were — but from an unexpected peculiarity in the material employed, when brought together in so large a mass as was necessary for Mr. Nasmyth's purpose. It seems that wrought iron, so tractable under all ordinary conditions of working, cannot be welded together in very large masses without undergoing a change in its molecular arrangement, exceedingly injurious to its tenacity. As we understand the explanation we have received on this point, an immense mass of iron, like that which Mr. Nasmyth has welded together, continues so long in an incandescent and soft state, that a process analogous to crystallization takes place within its substance, whereby the fibrous texture, from which it derives its tenacity is destroyed, and it becomes even less capable than cast-iron of resisting the explosion of a heavy charge of gunpowder. We understand that, in addition to the unfavorable result obtained by Mr. Nasmyth at Patricroft, another experiment of a similar nature, made under the direction of government, has proved a complete failure from the peculiarity in the material to which we have alluded; and a large gun which had been completed was found utterly unfit for use. Indeed, we believe it burst into many pieces on the first trial. Mr. Nasmyth's experiment has consequently been abandoned." *

The explosion of the large wrought iron gun on board the United States ship Princeton, some years since, was doubtless owing to the same cause.

Concussion alone, if long continued, will produce this change. A small bar of good tough iron was suspended and struck continually with small hand hammers, so as to keep up a constant vibration. The bar, after this experiment had been continued for some considerable time, became so exceedingly brittle, that it entirely fell to pieces, under the light blows of the hand hammers, presenting throughout its structure a highly crystalline appearance.

The cold hammering of railroad axles sometimes produces crystallization in the same manner as in the experiment just

* Manchester (England) Guardian.

cited. In order to test this Mr. Nasmyth subjected two pieces of cable bolt iron to one hundred and sixty blows between sways, and afterwards annealed one of the pieces for a few hours. The unannealed piece broke with five or six blows of the hammer, showing a crystalline fracture, while the annealed piece was bent double under a great number of blows, and exhibited a fine fibrous texture.

The shocks which the axles of road vehicles experience in use sometimes occasions this change, though the process must be very slow, when compared with that of railway axles. The wheels of cars and locomotives being fixed to the axle, and the axle rotating is much more liable to this change from various causes. Where the wheel is of cast-iron, the different vibrations of the two different materials seem to facilitate this change, and in this country, where cast-iron car wheels are to a great extent used, the fracture generally takes place close to the wheel. Owing to the rapid rotation of the axles they become highly magnetic, and there seems to be a close connection between magnetism and crystallization. The presence of steam seems to have an influence in producing this change, owing perhaps to the development of electricity, and this may have a great effect upon the axles of locomotives.

The severe winters of New England, as well from the action of frost on the iron axle, as from its effect in making the track rough, doubtless has a tendency to hasten the process of crystallization, and to produce fracture in axles affected by this change. We have known of the fracture of the axles of the driving wheels of two locomotives occurring on one road in New England, in one week during the month of February, 1856. One of them, which we had an opportunity to examine was broken close to the wheel, and the whole surface from the centre to within an eighth of an inch of the circumference presented a bright granulated appearance; a narrow rim extending round the whole axle looked smooth and of a duller color, as though it had been fractured for some time.

From the fact that this process of crystallization appears to begin in the centre of the axle, and from a belief that the effect of the blows and concussions which an axle receives, would be greatly diminished if the axle was made hollow, this plan has been tried upon several English roads, with a highly encouraging result. A hollow and a solid axle have been run hot in a lathe for two hours without oil, at a speed corresponding to twenty miles an hour travelling: the solid journal broke off, with 179 blows, quite short and crystalline, but the hollow journal would not break transversely, and split longitudinally in several places with 400 blows, without any appearance of change in the texture of the iron.

There seems to be no doubt that under certain circumstances wrought iron is liable to undergo a change by which its strength and tenacity are destroyed, and that railway axles are in a special manner liable to this change. Some of the causes or supposed causes of it, we have briefly alluded to; not with sufficient fulness perhaps, to afford much valuable practical information, but enough so, we trust, to lead others, with better opportunities and greater abilities, to investigate this subject, so important in its bearings both on the safe and the economical working of railroads.

Ordinances of the French Government, of the 22d and 23d May, 1843, relative to steam-engines.

These ordinances relate to the manufacture and establishment of steam-boilers; that is, to licenses for their use, to the tests they must be subjected to, to the thickness of the boilers, to the means of safety, (valves, gauges, supply-pumps, indicators of the level of water,) to the places in which they are used, and to the surveillance of the government. These ordinances comprise also the rules relative to the use of engines in mines, and to movable and locomotive engines.

What follows relating to steam-boilers is taken mostly from these ordinances.

Thickness of steam-boilers of iron plate or copper. This thickness is determined by the following formula.

$$e = 1.8\,d\,(n - 1) + 3;\ n = 1 + \frac{e - 3}{1.8\,d},$$

e = thickness of the boiler plate in millimetres,

d = diameter of the boiler in metres,

n = absolute tension of steam in the boiler. The effective pressure is $n - 1$.

The thickness of iron or copper plate for boilers ought never to exceed fifteen millimetres, — nine sixteenths of an inch; if on account of the size of the boiler, or the great pressure of the steam, a greater thickness would be required, a number of separate boilers of less diameter must be substituted for it. When a part of the boiler presents a plane surface, the thickness of this part must be increased.

The ordinance gives no rule for the thickness of cast-iron boilers, but according to the instructions annexed, every cylindrical boiler of cast-iron should be considered suspicious, the thickness of which is not at least five times that prescribed for a boiler of the same size in plate iron or copper.

As boiler plate iron is not found of all thicknesses, manufacturers make use of only a certain number of thicknesses, but these are always greater than those prescribed by law.

Tests for boilers. No steam-boiler can be put in use in any establishment whatever, without having been previously tested, by means of a water force-pump, with a pressure threefold that to be used, where the boiler is made of iron or copper plate, and fivefold when it is of cast-iron.

No steam-engine or boiler can be sold by the manufacturer, unless it has been subjected to the above tests. These tests are made at the shop, on the demand of the manufacturer, under the orders of the prefect, by the engineers of mines, or in their absence, by the engineers of bridges and roads. The tests are repeated at the place where the boilers or engines are to be used; 1st. If the proprietor demands it; 2d. If it has suffered any marked injury either in moving or putting it up; 3d. If there have been any modifications or alterations of it after the test at the shop.

Boilers or steam-engines, imported from other countries, must be provided with the same means of safety, as engines or boilers made in France, and must undergo the same tests. These tests are made at the place pointed out by the importer.

Licenses for the establishment of steam-engines and boilers. Steam-engines and boilers, whether high or low pressure, which are used in any other place than in mines, cannot be put in use, without a license from the prefect of the department, in conformity with the decree of the 15th October, 1810, relating to unhealthy and dangerous establishments.

The request for a license must be addressed to the prefect, and must show : —

1st. The maximum pressure of steam, under which the engine or boiler is to work, expressed in atmospheres and decimal parts of atmospheres.

2d. The force of the engine, expressed in horse-powers.

3d. The form of the boilers, their capacity and that of their tubes, expressed in cubic metres.

4th. The situation in which they are to be placed, and the distance from any buildings belonging to other persons, or from the public way.

5th. The nature of the fuel employed.

6th. The kind of work done by the engine.

A plan of the locality, and a geometrical sketch of the boiler must be sent with the request.

The prefect sends immediately the request for a license, with the plans, to the sub-prefect of the *arrondissement*, to be transmitted to the mayor of the *commune*, who proceeds immediately to an investigation *de commodo et incommodo*; this investigation is continued for ten days. Five days after its termination, the mayor addresses the *proces verbal* of the investigation, with his own opinion on the case, to the sub-prefect, who, after the same delay, transmits the whole, with his opinion, to the prefect. After a delay of fifteen days, in which the prefect has taken the opinion of the engineer of mines, or in his absence, of the engineer of bridges and roads, he decides upon the license.

Any one having been refused a license, by the prefect, can appeal to the council of State.

Safety-valves. Two safety-valves are fitted to the upper part of each boiler, one at each end. Each valve is loaded with a single weight acting either directly, or by means of a lever, upon it. Each weight is stamped, and where a lever is used, that is stamped also. The weight and the length of the lever are determined by a decree of the prefect.

The maximum load of each safety-valve is fixed by multiplying 1,033 by the number of atmospheres measuring the effective pressure, and by the number of square centimetres in the orifice covered by the valve. The result obtained is in kilogrammes.

The diameter of safety-valves is found by the formula,

$$d = 2.6 \sqrt{\frac{s}{n - 0.12}},$$

$d =$ diameter of the safety-valves in centimetres,

s. heating surface of the boiler, expressed in square metres,

n. absolute pressure in atmospheres.

Experiment has shown that a single valve, whose orifice has the diameter fixed by the above formula, is sufficient to discharge all the steam which can form in the boiler under a pressure of n atmospheres, when the fire is most active. Thus, when a boiler is furnished with two valves, having the prescribed dimensions and working well, there is no reason to fear that the steam will exceed the assigned limits of pressure, except, perhaps, in the case, where the water, through faults in the means of supply, is brought in contact with highly heated surfaces.

The new ordinances dispense with the use of the fusible plug, which was previously insisted upon.

Gauges. Every steam-boiler must be furnished with a mercurial gauge, graduated in atmospheres and decimal fractions of atmospheres, so as to show at once the pressure of the steam in the boiler. The pipe leading to the gauge must be fixed directly upon the boiler, and the gauge must be placed so as to be readily seen by the fireman. A line distinctly marked upon each scale, should indicate the level beyond which the mercury should not pass.

The Metallic Gauge of M. Bourdon is very convenient, and not easily broken. All locomotives are furnished with them. The government ordered a number of gauges of Mr. Bourdon for purposes of testing, graduated to eighteen atmospheres, and on the 26th August, 1852, one was sent to all engineers employed in the surveillance of steam-engines, for the purpose of testing all gauges used upon boilers.

Feed pumps for steam-boilers. Every steam-boiler must be furnished with a feed pump, well constructed and in good condition, and with all things necessary for a perfect supply of water.

The proper water-level in each boiler should be indicated on the outside by a line distinctly traced on the boiler or wall of the furnace. This line, which is called, the line of water-level, is at least a decimetre (3.9 inches) above the highest part of the tubes or passage ways for the flame and smoke.

Locomotive engines. The regulations relating to stationary engines apply to locomotives with the following exceptions.

The safety-valves of locomotive engines may be loaded by means of springs so arranged as to show, in kilogrammes and decimal fractions of kilogrammes, the pressure exerted against the valves.

No locomotive can be worked without a permit from the prefect of the department in which its starting point is situated.

The request for a permit must make known the facts indicated in the first and third clauses of the request for a license for the use of a stationary engine, and the name of the locomotive, and the service for which it is designed.

The name of the engine must be engraved on a plate fixed upon the boiler.

The prefect, after taking the advice of the engineer of mines, or in his absence, of the engineer of bridges and roads, gives, if he sees fit, the permit.

In this permit are shown: —

1st. The name of the engine, and the service for which it is designed.

2d. The maximum pressure (in number of atmospheres) of steam allowed.

3d. The diameter of the safety-valves.

4th. The capacity of the boilers.

5th. The diameter of the cylinders and the stroke of the pistons.

6th. The name of its manufacturer, and the year in which it was built.*

* Translated from Aide Memoire des Ingenieurs, des Architectes, etc., par J. Claudel, Paris, 1854.

E.

STATISTICS OF RAILROAD ACCIDENTS.

We have compiled the following table from the returns of the railroad corporations in Massachusetts to the legislature of that State. It includes all the accidents which have been reported for nine years extending from 1846 to 1854.

TABLE OF PERSONS killed and seriously injured on Massachusetts railroads from 1846 to 1854, inclusive.

	PASSENGERS.		EMPLOYES.		OTHERS.	
	Killed.	Wounded.	Killed.	Wounded.	Killed.	Wounded.
Explosions of locomotive boilers,			4			
Running off the track, . . .	6	10	12	7		
Collisions, ...	23	77	9	18		
Getting on and off trains while in motion, ...	28	25	13	5	7	2
Run over at grade crossings, .			1		42	27
Run over while walking or lying on the track, ...			11		164	45
Falling from trains, ...	13	2	43	12	6	
Striking objects while on the train,		5	57	23	4	
Making up of trains, . . .			29	16	1	1
Breaking of wheel or axle, .	6	5	1			
Breaking down of a bridge, . .			1			
	76	124	181	81	224	75

Four explosions of the boilers of locomotives are reported in these returns, by each of which one person was killed, but no details are given of the circumstances under which any of them occurred.

Passenger cars have been thrown from the track, according to these reports, in five instances; once by the fracture of a brake and its falling on the track — once by the breaking of the axle of a tender — once by the breaking of the centre shaft of the tender — once by a misplaced switch — once by running over a cow on the track.

Engines have been reported as having been thrown off in four instances; from the breaking of a switch; from a rock rolling down the slope on the track; and in two instances the cause is not given.

Freight trains have been reported as having been thrown off twice: once from the rails being up for repairs without being properly signalized, and once from the breaking of an axle.

Gravel trains have been reported as having been thrown off in two instances; once from obstructions maliciously placed on the track, and once from the fracture of a brake iron and the brake catching in the point of a frog.

There have been twenty-seven collisions; nine between two passenger trains, in two of which nineteen persons were killed, and fifty-seven persons wounded. In five of these cases no details are given and no cause assigned. In one the signals were not seen or not given. One was of a train overtaking another in a severe snow-storm, another in a dark foggy night, and another was caused by a misplaced switch turning a train upon another standing on a side track. Four cases have occurred of collisions between passenger trains and freight cars standing on a side track, occasioned by the switch having been set wrong. Two passenger trains have been struck by other trains at railroad crossings, and one passenger train was run into by a freight train, while obstructed by snow.

Analysis of accidents which occurred in Belgium, France, England, and Germany, during five years commencing August 1st, 1840.

	Fatal.	Total.
Belgium, ...	35	100
England, ...	300	1,500
France, ...	71	220
Germany, ...	11	22
	417	1,842

Passengers killed from their own fault.

Belgium, ...	1	in	670,000
England, ...	1	"	869,000
France, ...	1	"	2,157,000
Germany, ...	1	"	25,000,000

Officials killed or wounded from their own neglect.

Belgium, ...	1	in	280,000
England, ...	1	"	300,000
France, ...	1	"	5,000,000
Germany, ...	1	"	9,000,000

Persons killed by defective management.

Belgium, ...	1	in	1,690,764
England, ...	1	"	852,416
France, ...	1	"	3,565,996
Germany, ...	1	"	12,252,858 *

* Berlin Railway Year-Book, quoted in Civil Engineers' and Architects' Journal.

www.ingramcontent.com/pod-product-compliance
Lightning Source LLC
LaVergne TN
LVHW021359110826
845150LV00007B/1709

* 9 7 8 1 4 2 5 5 1 3 2 0 7 *